Quest for God

Dec 1987

Quest
for
God

Studies in Prayer and Symbolism

ABRAHAM JOSHUA HESCHEL

Crossroad · New York

1986
The Crossroad Publishing Company
370 Lexington Avenue, New York, NY 10017

Printed in the United States of America

Library of Congress Catalog Card No.: 81-70795

ISBN 0-8245-0436-4

Contents

v

Acknowledgments

I wish to acknowledge with thanks the permission granted by the following for the use of material of mine:

The Review of Religion, published by Columbia University Press, for the article on "Prayer" which appeared in Volume 9, No. 2, January 1945, issue and here appears as Chapter 1, "The Inner World," and for which copyright has been assigned to me.

The Rabbinical Assembly of America for the article "The Spirit of Prayer" which appeared in *The Proceedings of the Rabbinical Assembly of America*, 1953, and here is expanded in

Chapter 3, "Spontaneity Is the Goal," and for which copyright has been assigned to me.

The Central Conference of American Rabbis for the article "Toward an Understanding of Halacha" which appeared in the *Year Book of the Central Conference of American Rabbis,* Volume LXIII, and here is Chapter 4, "Continuity Is the Way."

Hebrew Union College for the article "The Meaning of This Hour," which appeared in a 1943 issue of *The Hebrew Union College Bulletin.*

Farrar, Straus & Young to quote excerpts from my book, *Man Is Not Alone,* as indicated.

Chapter 3, "Spontaneity Is the Goal," and Chapter 4, "Continuity Is the Way," were originally read as papers in June 1953 at the annual conventions of the Rabbinical Assembly of America in Atlantic City, New Jersey, and the Central Conference of American Rabbis in Estes Park, Colorado, respectively.

The substance of Chapter 5, "Symbolism," was originally delivered as a paper at the Institute for Religious and Social Studies at the Jewish Theological Seminary of America and is included in *Religious Symbolism,* edited by F. Ernest Johnson, published by the Institute, New York, 1954.

My sincere thanks are due to Rabbi Jacob Riemer for his assistance in the preparation of this manuscript for the press.

A. J. H.

Preface

There was never a time in which the need for self-expression was so much stressed. Yet, there was never a time in which self-expression was so rarely achieved; in which there was so much pressure to adjust oneself to conventions, clichés, to vogue and standardization. The self is silent; words are dead, and prayer is a forgotten language.

Man cannot pour his heart into a vacuum. If words are artificial signs; if meaning is but an invention; if there is no echo to the anguish of a tortured world; if man is alone; if the world moves in a vacuum, of what ultimate worth is all expression?

Man has become a forgotten thing. We know his desires, his whims, his failings; we do not know his ultimate commitment. We understand what he *does,* we do not understand what he *means.* We stand in awe of many things; we do not know what we stand for.

We are losing the power for self-expression, because genuine self-expression is *an answer to an ultimate question,* but we do not hear the ultimate question any more. We have lost any understanding for man's supreme concern, because such understanding is found not through self-inspection but through self-attachment to Him who is concerned with man.

To be sensitive to the ultimate question one must have the ability to surpass the self, the ability to know that the self is more than the self; that our highest concern is not our own concern; that our supreme standard is not expediency.

We are forfeiting the power to transcend the self and have become unable to transcend the mind. There is such an abundance of the here and the now, such plenitude of the given and the conceived that our mind has lost itself in the world. All we can trust in is the work of our hands, the product of our minds, and what lies beyond it is considered an illegitimate fancy. The world to us consists of instruments, of tools, and the supreme ideas are symbols only. *God is a name but no reality.* The standard of action is expediency, and God, too, is for the sake of our satisfaction.

Now, this seems to be a fact: God is of no concern to us. But there is another startling fact. His being of no concern to us has become a profound concern. We are concerned with our lack of concern.

God may be of no concern to man, but man is of much concern to God. The only way to discover this is the ultimate way, the way of worship. For worship is a way of living, a way of seeing the world in the light of God. To worship is to rise to a higher level of existence, to see the world from the point of view of God. In worship we discover that the ultimate way is not to have a symbol but *to be a symbol,* to stand for the divine. The ultimate way is to sanctify thoughts, to sanctify time, to consecrate words, to hallow deeds. The study of the word of God is an example of the sanctification of thought; the Seventh Day is an example of the sanctification of time; prayer is an example of the consecration of words; observance is an example of the hallowing of deeds.

We have lost the power to pray because we have lost the sense of His reality. All we do is done through symbols. We live for tools, we think in signs. What we do is for the sake of something else. It is therefore important that we pay attention to the role and meaning of symbols.

God is of no importance unless He is of supreme importance. It is hard to define religion; it is hard to place its wealth of meaning into the frame of a single sentence. But surely one thing may be said negatively: *religion is not expediency.* If all our actions are guided by one consideration, how best to serve our personal interests, it is not God whom we serve but the self. True, the self has its legitimate claims and interests; the persistent denial of the self, the defiance of one's own desire for happiness is not what God demands. But to remember that the love of God is for all men, for all creatures; to remember His love and His claim to love in making a decision—this is the way He wants us to live. To worship God is to forget the self. It is in such instants of worship that man acts as a symbol of Him.

Of all things we do prayer is the least expedient, the least worldly, the least practical. This is why prayer is an act of self-purification. This is why prayer is an ontological necessity.

We live through one of the great hours of history. The false gods are crumbling, and the hearts are hungry for the voice of God. But the voice has been stifled. To recapture the echo, we must be honest in our willingness to listen, we must be unprejudiced in our readiness to understand.

What goes on in the depth of our lives has a profound effect upon the international situation. Others may suffer from degradation by poverty; we are threatened by degradation through power. Power corrupts, and it is only the acceptance of the spirit of God that saves, that prevents disaster, that ennobles both body and soul.

The acceptance of the spirit is prayer—prayer as a way of insight, not as a way of speaking. Prayer may not save us, but prayer makes us worth saving.

Of all the sacred acts, first comes prayer. Religion is not "what man does with his solitariness." Religion is what man does with the presence of God. And the spirit of God is present whenever we are willing to accept it. True, God is hiding His face in our time, but He is hiding because we are evading Him.

A. J. H.

Quest for God

1

The Inner World

The Sigh

About a hundred years ago, Rabbi Isaac Meir Alter of Ger pondered over the question of what a certain shoemaker of his acquaintance should do about his morning prayer. His customers were poor men who owned only one pair of shoes. The shoemaker used to pick up their shoes at a late evening hour, work on them all night and part of the morning, in order to deliver them before their owners had to go to work. When should the shoemaker say his morning prayer? Should he pray quickly the first thing in the morning, and then go back to work? Or should he let the appointed hour of prayer go by and, every once in a while, raising his hammer from the shoes, utter a sigh: "Woe unto me, I haven't prayed yet!"? Perhaps that sigh is worth more than prayer itself.

We, too, face this dilemma of wholehearted regret or perfunctory fulfillment. Many of us regretfully refrain from habitual prayer, waiting for an urge that is complete, sudden, and unexampled. But the unexampled is scarce, and perpetual refraining can easily grow into a habit. We may even come to forget what to regret, what to miss.

The Ability to Answer

We do not refuse to pray. We merely feel that our tongues are tied, our minds inert, our inner vision dim, when we are about to enter the door that leads to prayer. We do not refuse to pray; we abstain from it. We ring the hollow bell of selfishness rather than absorb the stillness that surrounds the world, hovering over all the restlessness and fear of life—the secret stillness that precedes our birth and succeeds our death. Futile self-indulgence brings us out of tune with the gentle song of nature's waiting, of mankind's striving for salvation. Is not listening to the pulse of wonder worth silence and abstinence from self-assertion? Why do we not set apart an hour of living for devotion to God by surrendering to stillness? We dwell on the edge of mystery and ignore it, wasting our souls, risking our stake in God. We constantly pour our inner light away from Him, setting up the thick screen of self between Him and us, adding more shadows to the darkness that already hovers between Him and our wayward reason. Accepting surmises as dogmas, and prejudices as solutions, we ridicule the evidence of life for what is more than life. Our mind has ceased to be sensitive to the wonder. Deprived of the power of devotion to what is more important than our individual fate, steeped in passionate anxiety to survive, we lose sight of what fate is, of what living is. Rushing through the

4

ecstasies of ambition, we only awake when plunged into dread or grief. In darkness, then, we grope for solace, for meaning, for prayer.

But there is a wider voluntary entrance to prayer than sorrow and despair—the opening of our thoughts to God. We cannot make Him visible to us, but we can make ourselves visible to Him. So we open our thoughts to Him—feeble our tongues, but sensitive our hearts. We see more than we can say. The trees stand like guards of the Everlasting; the flowers like signposts of His goodness—only *we* have failed to be testimonies to His presence, tokens of His trust. How could we have lived in the shadow of greatness and defied it?

Mindfulness of God rises slowly, a thought at a time. Suddenly we are there. Or is He here, at the margin of our soul? When we begin to feel a qualm of diffidence lest we hurt what is holy, lest we break what is whole, then we discover that He is not austere. He answers with love our trembling awe. Repentant of forgetting Him even for a while, we become sharers of gentle joy; we would like to dedicate ourselves forever to the unfoldment of His final order.

To pray is to take notice of the wonder, to regain a sense of the mystery that animates all beings, the divine margin in all attainments. Prayer is *our* humble *answer* to the inconceivable surprise of living. It is all we can offer in return for the mystery by which we live. Who is worthy to be present at the constant unfolding of time? Amidst the meditation of mountains, the humility of flowers—wiser than all alphabets—clouds that die constantly for the sake of His glory, *we* are hating, hunting, hurting. Suddenly we feel ashamed of our clashes and complaints in the face of the tacit glory in nature. It is so embarrassing to live! How strange we are in the world, and how presumptuous our doings! Only one response can maintain us: gratefulness for witnessing the wonder, for the gift of our unearned right to serve, to adore, and to fulfill. It is gratefulness which makes the soul great.

However, we often lack the strength to be grateful, the courage to answer, the ability to pray. To escape from the mean and penurious, from calculating and scheming, is at times the parching desire of man. Tired of discord, he longs to escape from his own mind—and for the peace of prayer. How good it is to wrap oneself in prayer, spinning a deep softness of gratitude to God around all thoughts, enveloping oneself in the silken veil of song! But how can man draw song out of his heart if his consciousness is a woeful turmoil of fear and ambition? He has nothing to offer but disgust, and the weariness of wasting the soul. Accustomed to winding strands of thoughts, to twisting phrases in order to be successful, he is incapable of finding simple, straight words. His language abounds in traps and decoys, in shams and tricks, in gibes and sneers. In the teeth of such powerful distractions, he has to focus all the powers of his mind on one concern. In the midst of universal agitation, how can there be tranquillity?

Trembling in the realization that we are a blend of modesty and insolence, of self-denial and bias, we beseech God for rescue, for help in the control of our thoughts, words, and deeds. We lay all our forces before Him. Prayer is arrival at the border. The dominion is Thine. Take away from me all that may not enter Thy realm.

The Essence of Spiritual Living

As a tree torn from the soil, as a river separated from its source, the human soul wanes when detached from what is greater than itself. Without the holy, the good turns chaotic; without the good, beauty becomes accidental. It is the pattern of the impeccable which makes the average possible. It is the attachment to what is spiritually superior: loyalty to a sacred person or idea, devotion to a noble friend or teacher, love for a people or for mankind, which holds our inner life together. But any ideal, human, social, or artistic, if it forms a roof over all of life, shuts us off from the light. Even the palm of one hand may bar the light of the entire sun. Indeed, we must be open to the remote in order to perceive the near. Unless we aspire to the utmost, we shrink to inferiority.

Prayer is our attachment to the utmost. Without God in sight, we are like the scattered rungs of a broken ladder. To pray is to become a ladder on which thoughts mount to God to join the movement toward Him which surges unnoticed throughout the entire universe. We do not step out of the world when we pray; we merely see the world in a different setting. The self is not the hub, but the spoke of the revolving wheel. In prayer we shift the center of living from self-consciousness to self-surrender. God is the center toward which all forces tend. He is the source, and we are the flowing of His force, the ebb and flow of His tides.

Prayer takes the mind out of the narrowness of self-interest, and enables us to see the world in the mirror of the holy. For when we betake ourselves to the extreme opposite of the ego, we can behold a situation from the aspect of God. Prayer is a way to master what is inferior in us, to discern between the signal and the trivial, between the vital and the futile, by taking counsel with what we know about the will of God, by seeing our fate in proportion to God. Prayer clarifies our hope and intentions. It helps us discover our true aspirations, the pangs we ignore, the longings we forget. It is an act of self-purification, a quarantine for the soul. It gives us the opportunity to be honest, to say what we believe, and to stand for what we say. For the accord of assertion and conviction, of thought and conscience, is the basis of all prayer.

Prayer teaches us what to aspire to. So often we do not know what to cling to. Prayer implants in us the ideals we ought to cherish. Redemption, purity of mind and tongue, or willingness to help, may hover as ideas before our mind, but the idea becomes a concern, something to long for, a goal to be reached, when we pray: "Guard my tongue from evil and my lips from speaking guile; and in the face of those who curse me, let my soul be silent."[1]

[1] From the daily liturgy.

Prayer is the essence of spiritual living. Its spell is present in every spiritual experience. Its drive enables us to delve into what is what beneath our beliefs and desires, and to emerge with a renewed taste for the infinite simplicity of the good. On the globe of the microcosm the flow of prayer is like the Gulf Stream, imparting warmth to all that is cold, melting all that is hard in our life. For even loyalties may freeze to indifference if detached from the stream which carries the strength to be loyal. How often does justice lapse into cruelty, and righteousness into hypocrisy. Prayer revives and keeps alive the rare greatness of some past experience in which things glowed with meaning and blessing. It remains important, even when we ignore it for a while, like a candlestick set aside for the day. Night will come, and we shall again gather round its tiny flame. Our affection for the trifles of living will be mixed with longing for the comfort of all men.

However, prayer is no panacea, no substitute for action. It is, rather, like a beam thrown from a flashlight before us into the darkness. It is in this light that we who grope, stumble, and climb, discover where we stand, what surrounds us, and the course which we should choose. Prayer makes visible the right, and reveals what is hampering and false. In its radiance, we behold the worth of our efforts, the range of our hopes, and the meaning of our deeds. Envy and fear, despair and resentment, anguish and grief, which lie heavily upon the heart, are dispelled like shadows by its light.

Sometimes prayer is more than a light before us; it is a light within us. Those who have once been resplendent with this light find little meaning in speculations about the efficacy of prayer. A story is told about a Rabbi who once entered heaven in a dream. He was permitted to approach the temple of Paradise where the great sages of the Talmud, the Tannaim, were spending their eternal lives. He saw that they were just sitting around tables studying the Talmud. The disappointed Rabbi wondered, "Is this all there is to Paradise?" But suddenly he heard a voice, "You are mistaken. The Tannaim are not in Paradise. Paradise is in the Tannaim."

8

Man's Ultimate Aspiration

In those souls in which prayer is a rare flower, enchanting, surprising, it seems to come to pass by the lucky chance of misfortune, as an inevitable or adventitious by-product of affliction. But suffering is not the source of prayer. A motive does not bring about an act as a cause produces an effect; it merely stimulates the potential into becoming an actuality. Peril or want may clear the ground for its growth, stubbing up the weeds of self-assurance, ridding the heart of the hard and obdurate, but it can never raise prayer.

To a farmer about to prepare a seedbed, the prerequisite for his undertaking is not the accidental need of a crop. His need of food does not endow him with skill in cultivating the earth; it merely affords the stimulus and purpose for his undertaking. It is his knowledge, his possession of the idea of tillage, which enables him to raise crops. The same principle applies to prayer. The natural loyalty of living, fertilized by faith saved through a lifetime, is the soil on which prayer can grow. Laden with secret fertility and patient discreetness concerning things to be and things forever unknown, the soil of the soul nourishes and holds the roots of prayer. But the soil by itself does not produce crops. There must also be the idea of prayer to make the soul yield its amazing fruit.

The idea of prayer is based upon the assumption of man's ability to accost God, to lay our hopes, sorrows, and wishes before Him. But this assumption is not an awareness of a particular ability with which we are endowed. We do not feel that we possess a magic power of speaking to the Infinite; we merely witness the wonder of prayer, the wonder of man addressing himself to the Eternal. Contact with Him is not our achievement. It is a gift, coming down to us from on high like a meteor, rather than rising up like a rocket. Before the words of prayer come to the lips, the mind must believe in God's willingness to draw near to us, and in our ability to clear the path for His approach. Such belief is the idea that leads us toward prayer.

Prayer is not a soliloquy. But is it a dialogue with God?[2] Does man address Him as person to person? It is incorrect to describe prayer by analogy with human conversation; we do not communicate with God. We only make ourselves communicable to Him. Prayer is an emanation of what is most precious in us toward Him, the outpouring of the heart before Him. It is not a relationship between person and person, between subject and subject, but an endeavor to become the object of His thought.

Prayer is like the light from a burning glass in which all the rays that emanate from the soul are gathered to a focus. There are hours when we are resplendent with the glowing awareness of our share in His secret interests on earth. We pray. We are carried forward to Him who is coming close to us. We endeavor to divine His will, not merely His command. Prayer is an answer to God: "Here am I. And this is the record of my days. Look into my heart, into my hopes and my regrets." We depart in shame and joy. Yet prayer never ends, for faith endows us with a bold craving that He draw near to us and approach us as a father—not only as a ruler; not only through our walking in His ways, but through His entering into our ways. The purpose of prayer is to be brought to His attention, to be listened to, to be understood by Him; not to know Him, but to *be known* to Him. To pray is to behold life not only as a result of His power, but as a concern of His will, or to strive to make our life a divine concern. For the ultimate aspiration of man is not to be a master, but an object of His knowledge. To live "in the light of His countenance," to become a thought of God—this is the true career of man.

But are we worthy of being known, of entering into His mercy, of being a matter of concern to Him? It seems as if the meaning of prayer lies in man's aspiration to be thought of by God as

[2]Prayer is defined as a dialogue with God by Clement of Alexandria. See Max Pohlenz, *Die Stoa,* Geschichte einer geistigen Bewegung, Goettingen, 1948, Vol. I, p. 423.

one who is thinking of Him. Man waxes in God when serving the sacred, and wanes when he betrays his task. Man lives in His mind when He abides in man's life.

There is no human misery more strongly felt than the state of being forsaken by God. Nothing is so terrible as rejection by Him. It is a horror to live deserted by God, and effaced from His mind. The fear of being forgotten even for an instant is a powerful spur to a pious man to bring himself to the attention of God, to keep his life *worth* being known to Him. He prefers to be smitten by His punishment rather than to be left alone. In all his prayers he begs, explicitly or implicitly, "Do not forsake me, O Lord."

The man who betrays Him day after day, drunk with vanity, resentment, or reckless ambition, lives in a ghostly mist of misgivings. Having ruined love with greed, he is still wondering about the lack of tenderness in his own life. His soul contains a hiding-place for an escaping conscience. He has torn his ties to God into shreds of shrieking dread, and his mind remains dull and callous. Spoiler of his own lot, he walks the earth a skeleton of a soul, raving about missed delight.

God is not alone when discarded by man. But man is alone. To avoid prayer constantly is to force a gap between man and God which can widen into an abyss. But sometimes, awakening on the edge of despair to weep, and arising from forgetfulness, we feel how yearning moves in softly to become the lord of a restless breast, and we pass over the gap with the lightness of a dream.

The Nature of *Kavanah*

Commentators have been puzzled at the passage in the *amidah* ("the silent prayer"), *"for Thou hearest in mercy the prayer of every mouth."* We would expect the phrase to be *"the prayer of every heart."* But the passage, we are told, is intended to remind us that it is the mercy of God to accept even prayers that come only from the mouth as lip-service, without inner devotion.[3] However, this remark in no way denies the principle that *kavanah*, or inner participation, is indispensable to prayer. It is a principle that found a precise expression in the medieval saying: "Prayer without *kavanah* is like a body without a soul."

Yet, what is the nature of *kavanah* or inner participation? Is it paying attention to the context of the fixed texts? Thinking? Prayer is not thinking. To the thinker, God is an object; to the man who prays, He is the subject. Awaking in the presence of God, we strive not to acquire objective knowledge, but to deepen the mutual allegiance of man and God. What we want is not to know Him, but to be known to Him; not to form judgments about Him, but to be judged by Him; not to make the world an object of our mind, but to let the world come to His attention, to augment His, rather than our knowledge. We endeavor to disclose ourselves to the Sustainer of all, rather than to enclose the world in ourselves.

To most people, thinking is a thing that grows in the hothouse of logic, separated from the atmosphere of character and of everyday living. They consider it possible for a man to be unscrupulous and yet to write well about righteousness. Others may disagree with this view. However, all of us, mindful of the ancient distinction between lip-service and the service of the heart, agree that prayer is not a hothouse plant of temples, but a shoot that grows in the soil of life, springing from widespread roots hidden in all our needs and deeds. Vicious needs, wicked deeds, felt or committed today, are like rot cankering the roots of tomorrow's prayer. A hand used in crime is an axe laid to the roots of worship. In the words of Isaiah (1:15): "When ye spread forth your hands, I will hide my eyes from you; even though ye make many prayers, I will not listen; your hands are full of blood." Life is fashioned by prayer, and prayer is the quintessence of life.

The laws of science we comprehend as rational concepts in critical understanding, while the mercy and greatness of the

[3]Rabbi Menahem Lonzano, *Derech Hayim,* Lemberg, 1931, p. 101; Rabbi Aaron of Karlin, *Beth Aaron,* Brody, 1875, p. 285a.

12

Infinite we absorb as a mystery. Prayer is a spiritual source in itself. Though not born of an urge to learn, it often endows us with insights not attainable by speculation. It is in prayer that we obtain the subsidy of God for the failing efforts of our wisdom.

But prayer goes beyond the scope of emotion; it is the approach of the human to the transcendent. Prayer makes man a relative to the sublime, initiating him into the mystery. The will, at times, is an outsider to the sanctuary of the soul. It ushers in great things, but does not always control them. The will to pray opens the gates, but what enters is not its product. The will is not a creative, but an auxiliary power, the servant of the soul. Creative forces may be discharged, but not engendered, by the will. Thus, inclination to pray is not prayer. Deeper forces and qualities of the soul must be mobilized before prayer can be accomplished. To pray is to pull ourselves together, to pour our perception, volition, memory, thought, hope, feeling, dreams, all that is moving in us, into one tone. Not the words we utter, the service of the lips, but the way in which the devotion of the heart corresponds to what the words contain, the consciousness of speaking under His eyes, is the pith of prayer.

For neither the lips nor the brain are the limits of the scene in which prayer takes place. Speech and devotion are functions auxiliary to a metaphysical process. Common to all men who pray is the certainty that prayer is an act which makes the heart audible to God. Who would pour his most precious hopes into an abyss? Essential is the metaphysical rather than the physical dimension of prayer. Prayer is not a thought that rambles alone in the world, but an event that starts in man and ends in God. What goes on in our heart is a humble preliminary to an event in God.

The passage of hours, almost unnoticeable, but leaving behind the feeling of loss or omission, is either an invitation to despair or a ladder to eternity. This little time in our hands melts away ere it can be formed. Before our eyes man and maid, spring and splendor, slide into oblivion. However, there are hours that perish and hours that join the everlasting. Prayer is a crucible in which time is cast in the likeness of the eternal. Man hands over his time to God in the secrecy of single words. When anointed by prayer, his thoughts and deeds do not sink into nothingness, but merge into the endless knowledge of an all-embracing God. We yield our thoughts to Him who endowed us with a chain of days for the duration of life.

An Invitation to God

To many psychologists, prayer is but a function, a shadow cast by the circumstances of our lives, growing and diminishing in accordance with our various needs and wants. Consequently, to understand the nature of prayer, it is enough to become familiar with the various occasions on which it is offered. But is it possible to determine the value of a work of art by discovering the occasion of its creation? Assuming that we can ascertain whether Cervantes wrote his *Don Quixote* in order to pay his debts, or to attain fame and impress his friends, would that have any bearing upon either the intrinsic value or our appreciation of his art? Nor is the factor which induces a person to pray the essence of prayer. The essence is inherent in the act of prayer itself. It can be detected only inside the consciousness of man during the act of worship.

The drive toward practical consequences is not the force that inspires a person at the moment of his chanting praise to God. Even in supplication, the thought of aid or protection does not constitute the inner act of prayer. The hope of results may be the motive that leads the mind into prayer, but not the content which fills the worshiper's consciousness in the essential moment of prayer. The artist may give a concert for the sake of the promised remuneration, but, in the moment when he is passionately seeking with his fingertips the vast swarm of swift and secret sounds, the consideration of subsequent reward is far from his mind. His whole being is immersed in the music. The slightest shift of attention, the emergence of any ulterior motive, would break his intense concentration, and his single-minded devotion

14

would collapse, his control of the instrument would fail. Even an artisan can never be true to his task unless he is motivated by love of the work for its own sake. Only by wholehearted devotion to his trade, can he produce a consummate piece of craftsmanship. Prayer, too, is primarily *kavanah*, the yielding of the entire being to one goal, the gathering of the soul into focus.

The focus of prayer is not the self. A man may spend hours meditating about himself, or be stirred by the deepest sympathy for his fellow man, and no prayer will come to pass. Prayer comes to pass in a complete turning of the heart toward God, toward His goodness and power. It is the momentary disregard of our personal concerns, the absence of self-centered thoughts, which constitute the art of prayer. Feeling becomes prayer in the moment in which we forget ourselves and become aware of God. When we analyze the consciousness of a supplicant, we discover that it is not concentrated upon his own interests, but on something beyond the self. The thought of personal need is absent, and the thought of divine grace alone is present in his mind. Thus, in beseeching Him for bread, there is *one* instant, at least, in which our mind is directed neither to our hunger nor to food, but to His mercy. This instant is prayer.

We start with a personal concern and live to feel the utmost. For the fate of the individual is a counterpoint in a larger theme. In prayer we come close to hearing the eternal theme and discerning our place in it. It is as if our life were a seamless garment, continuous with the Infinite. Our poverty is His. His property is ours. Overwhelmed with awe of His share in our lives, we extend ourselves to Him, expose our goals to His goodness, exchange our will for His wisdom. For this reason, the analogy between prayer and petitioning another human being is like the analogy between the ocean and a cup of water. For the essence of prayer lies in man's self-transcending, in his surpassing the limits of what is human, in his relating the purely natural to the Divine.

Prayer is an invitation to God to intervene in our lives, to let His will prevail in our affairs; it is the opening of a window to Him in our will, an effort to make Him the Lord of our soul. We

15

submit our interests to His concern, and seek to be allied with what is ultimately right. Our approach to the holy is not an intrusion, but an answer. Between the dawn of childhood and the door of death, man encounters things and events out of which comes a whisper of truth, not much louder than stillness, but exhorting and persistent. Yet man listens to his fears and his whims, rather than to the gentle petitions of God. The Lord of the universe is suing for the favor of man, but man fails to realize his correlation. It is the disentanglement of our heart from cant, bias, and ambition, the staving in of the bulk of stupid conceit, the cracking of hollow self-reliance, that enables us to respond to this request for our service.

The purpose of prayer is not the same as the purpose of speech. The purpose of speech is to inform; the purpose of prayer is to partake.

In speech, the act and the content are not always contemporaneous. What we wish to communicate to others is usually present in our minds prior to the moment of communication. In contrast, the actual content of prayer comes into being in the moment of praying. For the true content of prayer, the true sacrifice we offer, is not the prescribed word which we repeat, but the response to it, the self-examination of the heart, the realization of what is at stake in living as a child of God, as a part of Israel. These elements which constitute the substance of prayer come into being within prayer.

Is it the outburst of eloquence which makes the infinite listen to our feeble voice? Prayer is not a sermon delivered to God. In oratory, as in any other work of art, we endeavor to lend an adequate form to an idea; we apply all our care to adjusting the form to the content. But in prayer it makes little difference whether we stammer or are eloquent.

Twice daily we try to impress upon our hearts the words, uttered in Hebrew, *Thou shalt love the Lord thy God with all thy heart, with all thy soul, with all thy might.* However, there are those who know the meaning but not the right pronunciation of these Hebrew words. Does perfect love depend upon the perfect pronunciation, upon proper articulation?

16

We read in the Song of Songs (2:4), *And his banner (digulo) over me is love (ahavah)*. "Rabbi Aha said: If an ignorant man reads 'hate' instead of love by saying for instance *we-ayabta* (and thou shalt hate) for *we-ahabta* (and thou shalt love), God says: 'His mistake (*dilugo*) is beloved to me.' "[4]

The quality of a speech is not judged by the good intention of the speaker but by the degree to which it succeeds to simplify an idea and to make it relevant to others. In contrast, the goal of prayer is to simplify the self and to make God relevant to oneself. Thus, prayer is judged not by standards of rhetoric but by the good intention, by the earnestness and intensity of the person.

Ultimately the goal of prayer is not to translate a word but to translate the self; not to render an ancient vocabulary in modern terminology, but to transform our thoughts into thoughts of prayer. Prayer is the soul's *imitation of the spirit*, of the spirit that is contained in the liturgical word.

Spiritual Ecstasy

The thirst for companionship, which drives us so often into error and adventure, indicates the intense loneliness from which we suffer. We are alone even with our friends. The smattering of understanding which a human being has to offer is not enough to satisfy our need of sympathy. Human eyes can see the foam, but not the seething at the bottom. In the hour of greatest agony we are alone. It is such a sense of solitude which prompts the heart to seek the companionship of God. He alone perceives the motives of our actions; He alone can be truly trusted. Prayer is confidence, unbosoming oneself to God. For man is incapable of being alone. His incurable, inconsolable loneliness forces him to look for things yet unattained, for people yet unknown. He often runs after a sop, but soon retires discontented from all

[4] *Midrash Rabba*, The Song of Songs, II, 13.

false or feeble companionship. Prayer may follow such retirement.

What is pride worth if it does not add to the glory of God? We forfeit our dignity when abandoning loyalty to what is sacred; our existence dwindles to trifles. We barter life for oblivion, and pay the price of toil and pain in the pursuit of aimlessness. Only the concern for our inalienable share in the unknown holds our inner life together. It enables us to grasp the utopia of faith, to divine what is desirable to God, aspiring to be, not only a part of nature, but a partner of God. The sacred is a necessity in our lives, and prayer is born of this necessity. Through prayer we sanctify ourselves, our feelings, our ideas. Everyday things become sacred when prayed for to God.

The privilege of praying is man's greatest distinction. For what is there in man to induce reverence, to make his life sacred and his rights inalienable? The possession of knowledge, wealth, or skill does not compose the dignity of man. A person possessing none of these gifts may still lay claim to dignity. Our reverence for man is aroused by something in him beyond his own and our reach, something that no one can deprive him of. It is his right to pray, his ability to worship, to utter the cry that can reach God: "If . . . they cry out to Me, I will surely hear their cry."[5]

The main ends of prayer are to move God, to let Him participate in our lives, and to interest ourselves in Him. What is the meaning of praise if not to make His concern our own? Worship is an act of inner agreement with God. We can only petition Him for things we need when we are sure of His sympathy for us. To praise is to feel God's concern; to petition is to let Him feel our concern. In prayer we establish a living contact with God, between our concern and His will, between despair and promise, want and abundance. We affirm our adherence by invoking His love.

Prayer is *spiritual ecstasy*. It is as if all our vital thoughts in fierce ardor would burst the mind to stream toward God. A keen single force draws our yearning for the utmost out of the seclu-

[5]Exodus 22:22. See p. 78.

18

sion of the soul. We try to see our visions in His light, to feel our life as His affair. We begin by letting the thought of Him engage our minds, by realizing His name and entering into a reverie which leads through beauty and stillness, from feeling to thought, and from understanding to devotion. For the coins of prayer bear the image of God's dreams and wishes for fear-haunted man.

At the beginning of all action is an inner vision in which things to be are experienced as real. Prayer, too, is frequently an inner vision, an intense dreaming for God—the reflection of the Divine intentions in the soul of man. We dream of a time "when the world will be perfected under the Kingship of God, and all the children of flesh will call upon Thy name, when Thou wilt turn unto Thyself all the wicked of the earth."[6] We anticipate the fulfillment of the hope shared by both God and man. To pray is to dream in league with God, to envision His holy visions.

[6]From the daily liturgy.

2

The Person
and the Word

The Dignity of Words

Studies about prayer are usually concerned with the person who prays—his feelings or motivations, with the text of prayer —its history, content or style, or with the theme of prayer—praise, petition or confession. Our concern here will be to explore the act of praying. This is our question: What is taking place when a person is praying?

It takes two things to make prayer come to pass: a person and a word. In scholarly studies, these two components appear as if they existed loosely one beside the other; each of them is separately discussed and independently classified. However, as long as person and word are apart, there is no praying. A word detached from the person is numb; a person detached from the word is illiterate. The very essence of prayer is in a blending of the two.

To be engaged in prayer and to be away from prayer are two different states of living and thinking. In the depth of the soul there is a distance between the two. The course of consciousness which a person pursues, the way of thinking by which he lives most of the time, are remote from the course and way of thinking peculiar to prayer. To be able to pray one must alter the course of consciousness, one must go through moments of disengagement, one must adjust oneself to another way and another atmosphere of thinking.

How does the change come to pass? How does a person who is away from prayer become a person who is engaged in prayer? Those who have dealt with the problem derive the act of prayer from certain mental, emotional or social impulses or conditions.[1] It is said, for example, that great joy or deep sorrow is the source of prayer. Yet, in stressing the psychological impulse or the sociological factor, we often lose sight of the fact that everyday prayer springs to a much greater degree from another source. It is in prayer itself that one becomes a praying man, and seldom before. One becomes a praying man by means of the *word*.

Consequently, in order to understand prayer, the relation between man and the word, its nature and function, must be seen clearly. How does the relation arise? How does man relate himself to the word? What does the word mean to him who prays?

We are all involved in many relationships, but these relationships are not all the same. They differ according to whether we deal with an animal or with a human being, with a plant or with a work of art, with a ritual object or with a tool. Now, what does the word mean to us? What is its status? What is its relevance?

Little do we think about the nature of words, though nowhere does the might of the spirit appear so openly, so directly, so explicitly, though nowhere is its power so tangibly present as in words.

[1]See above, p. 14.

24

What do most of us know about the substance of words? Estranged from the soil of the soul, our words do not grow as fruits of insights, but are found as sapless clichés, refuse in the backyard of intelligence. To the man of our age nothing is as familiar and nothing as trite as words. Of all things they are the cheapest, most abused and least regarded. They are the object of frequent defilement. We all live in them, feel in them, think in them, but failing to uphold their independent dignity, to respect their power and weight, they turn waif, elusive—a mouthful of dust.

Words have ceased to be commitments. Our sensitivity to their power is being constantly reduced. And bitter is the fate of those who forfeit completely the sense for their weight, for words when abused take vengeance on the abusers. Indeed, there can be no prayer without a sense for the dignity of words, without a degree of deference to what they stand for.

In acts of genuine expression, what goes on between the soul of man and the word of prayer is more than an act of employment, of using words as if they were tools. Here the soul and the word react upon each other; the word is a creative force.

Words are not made of paper. Words of prayer are repositories of the spirit. It is only after we kindle a light in the words that we are able to behold the riches they contain. It is only after we arrive within a word that we become aware of the riches our own souls contain.

Words Speak

We shall never be able to understand that the spirit is revealed in the form of words, unless we discover the vital truth that speech has power, that words are commitments.

Everyone feels the binding force of the uttered word, the reality of an oath, of a vow, of a promise. In making a pledge, in giving a word of honor, in uttering an oath or in entering an oral agreement, man learns to understand that the word is stronger than the will, that a word given exists independently and regardless of its relation and pertinence to him. It is a reality for him, something existing for itself. Without being clear about its meaning, he becomes alive to its power.

It is in such objectivity that the word stands before the praying man. The word of prayer is like a pledge in the making.

Words of prayer do not fade. They remain alive in the holy dimension. Words of prayer are commitments. We stand for what we utter. Prayer is the opposite of pretentiousness.

Words are more than signs, more than combinations of letters. Letters are one-dimensional and have only one function: to represent sounds. Words, on the other hand, have fullness and depth, they are multi-dimensional. It is true that we employ words to represent things or to let them carry our ideas and to convey them to others. Yet to say that words are nothing but mental beasts of burden would be the same as to see in the person who carries our luggage to the train nothing but a porter. The essence of a person is not in carrying luggage, and the essence of a word is not in its being a sign. Let us distinguish between substance and function, between the essential nature of a word and its function, the mode in which it is used by us.

Our understanding of the word is immediate. We do not appreciate a word by first realizing the thing or the idea it denotes and then coming back to the word. In uttering words, such as mountain or beauty it is not an image or a quality of things that is immediately reproduced in our minds. What we encounter is the word itself, its unique intensity, the complex of meanings which surround it and which exist far beyond its dictionary meaning, of its strict relation to the object of which it is a sign.

A word is a focus, a point at which meanings meet and from which meanings seem to proceed. In prayer, as in poetry, we turn to the words, not to use them as signs for things, but to see the things in the light of the words. In daily speech, it is usually we who speak words, but the words are silent. In poetry, in prayer, the words speak.

The forces of the word are ordinarily tamed. They must be

26

unleashed in order to come forth, in order to be perceived. The situation of the praying man is thus, from the beginning, no passive one. To begin to pray is to confront the word, to face its dignity, its singularity, and to sense its potential might. And it is the spiritual power of the praying man that makes manifest what is dormant in the text. The character of the act of prayer depends on the reciprocal relation between the person and the word.

It is not enough, therefore, to articulate a sound. Unless one understands that the word is stronger than the will; unless one knows how to approach a word with all the joy, the hope or the grief he owns, prayer will hardly come to pass. The words must not fall off our lips like dead leaves in the autumn. They must rise like birds out of the heart into the vast expanse of eternity.

When the heart, cooperating with the forces of faith against tumult and anxiety, succeeds in keeping alive the inner stillness, we feel how great and gentle words can be. Strength and glory come from their sounds. They soften the harshness of fear and unfold the wings of hope. Our thoughts, tiny and feeble, become powerful in their wake.

In our own civilization, in which so much is being done for the cause of the liquidation of language, the realm of prayer is like an arsenal for the spirit, where words are kept clean, holy, full of power to inspire and to keep us spiritually alive. Out of that arsenal we get the strength to save our faith, our appreciation of things eternal, from vanishing away.

In crisis, in moments of despair, a word of prayer is like a strap we take hold of when tottering in a rushing street car which seems to be turning over.

An Island in This World

Prayer, as said above, is an event that comes to pass between the soul of man and the word. It is from this point of view, that we have to distinguish between two main types of prayer:

prayer as *an act of expression* and prayer as *an act of empathy*.

The first type comes to pass when we feel the urge to set forth before God a personal concern. Here the concern, and even the mood and the desire to pray, come first; the word follows. It is the urge to pray that leads to the act of praying.

While it is true that the prayer of expression is a common and universal phenomenon, it is inaccurate to assume, as most people do, that prayer occurs primarily as an act of expression. The fact is that the more common type of prayer is *an act of empathy*. There need be no prayerful mood in us when we begin to pray. It is through our reading and feeling the words of the prayers, through the imaginative projection of our consciousness into the meaning of the words, and through empathy for the ideas with which the words are pregnant, that this type of prayer comes to pass. Here the word comes first, the feeling follows.

In the Book of Psalms some chapters begin with the words, *To David, a Psalm,* while others begin, *A Psalm to David.* The Talmud explains: when David began to sing and then the inspiration came to him it was *To David a Psalm;* when first the inspiration came to him and then he sang, it was *A Psalm to David.*[2]

In the prayer of empathy, we begin by turning to the words of the liturgy. At first, the words and their meaning seem to lie beyond the horizon of the mind. How remote is the meaning of *Blessed be Thou* to the thoughts in which we are usually immersed. We must, therefore, remember that the experience of prayer does not come all at once. It grows in the face of the word that comes ever more to light in its richness, buoyancy, and mystery. Gradually, going out to meet its meaning, we rise to the greatness of prayer. On the way to the word, on its slopes and ridges, prayer matures—we purify ourselves into beings who pray.

An island in this world are the words of prayer. Each time when arriving at the shore, we face the same hazards, the same strain, tension and risk. Each time the island must be conquered, as if we had never been there before, as if we were strangers

---

[2] *Pesahim,* 117a.

28

to the spirit. Rugged is the shore, and in the sight of majestic utterances we stand, seeking a kindred word on which to gain a foothold for our souls. The words we face are lofty, and the humble ones are concealed, beyond our reach. We must not be shaken. We must learn how to crawl, if we do not know how to leap. Prayer, as said above, does not complete itself in an instant, nor does it move on a level plane, but thrusts itself forward through depths and heights, through detours and byways. It runs its course as a gradually advancing action, from word to word, from thought to thought, from feeling to feeling. Arriving, we discover a level where words are treasures, where meanings lie hidden still to be mined. Restrained insights, slumbering emotions, the subdued voice of deeper knowledge bursts upon the mind.

The concepts which indicate the divine surpass the bounds of human consciousness. The words which tell of it exceed the power of the soul, and, over and above that, they demand an intensity of dedication which is rarely present. To name Him is a risk, a forcing of the consciousness beyond itself. To refer to Him, means almost to get outside oneself. Every praying person knows how serious an act the utterance of His name is, for the word is not a tool but a reflection of the object which it designates. We often discover that the word is greater than the mind. What we feel is so much less than what we say.

In the prayer of expression we often arrive at thoughts that lie beyond our power of expression. In the prayer of empathy we often arrive at words that lie beyond our power of empathy. It is in such tensions that our worship gains in strength and our knowledge in intuitive depth.

Genuine prayer is an event in which man surpasses himself. Man hardly comprehends what is coming to pass. Its beginning lies on this side of the word, but the end lies beyond all words. What is happening is not always brought about by the power of man. At times all we do is to utter a word with all our heart, yet it is as if we lifted up a whole world. It is as if someone unsuspectingly pressed a button and a gigantic wheel-work were stormily and surprisingly set in motion.

We do not turn the light of prayer on and off at will, as we control sober speculation; we are seized by the overwhelming spell of its grandeur. It is amazement, not understanding; awe, not reasoning; a challenge, a sweep of emotion, the tide of the spirit, a claim on our wills by the living will of God.

The service of prayer, the worship of the heart, fulfills itself not in the employment of words as a human expression but in the celebration of words as a holy reality. One is ashamed to open his experiences, to disclose his feelings before the face of God; only rarely does he fully overcome his inhibition. What he can do most easily is this: to capture the substance of the word with aroused attention and devotion and offer it with trembling. The power which streams from words unites itself with the elemental power that rises from the memory. Thoughts are being transcended, experiences of the past illumined, desires transformed. A thought becomes a wish, a wish a desire, a desire a demand, a demand an expectation, an expectation a vision. These steps represent at once stages of personal attitude as well as objective events.

Praying means to take hold of a word, the end, so to speak, of a line that leads to God. The greater the power, the higher the ascent in the word. But praying also means that the echo of the word falls like a plummet into the depth of the soul. The purer the readiness, so much the deeper penetrates the word.

An Answer of the Whole Person

Prayer, we all agree, is an outburst of the heart, an act of spontaneity and self-expression. But does not a liturgy that gives priority to the prayer of empathy lead to the stultification of spontaneity? Does not the adherence to a fixed pattern of the liturgy impair the element of inwardness, the role of self-expression?

The truth is that the absolute contrast between expression and empathy exists only in abstraction. In human experience they are intimately intertwined; the one cannot happen without the other. An act of empathy is involved in genuine expression, and profound empathy generates expression.

For is there such a thing as *absolute* self-expression, as expression without empathy? Self-expression involves the employment of means of expression such as word, color, tone, form. Now, is it possible to succeed in any effort of expression without bearing regard for the means of expression? To be able to put "the self" into words one must not only know the intricacies of the self but also the intricacies of the word; one must know how to solicit words that would reflect the concern of the self; one must know how to find words that are consonant with the self. Such skill is contingent upon an inner understanding of the singularity of words, upon empathy for their inner life. Adequate expression can never be achieved without the ability to commune with the means of expression, without the ability to partake of the substance of the words.

It is either short-sighted or vainglorious to assume that self-expression as such is the supreme goal of prayer. The supreme goal of prayer is to express God, to discover the self in relation to God.

In the light of eternity, it seems childish to maintain that our supreme goal is to express the self. What is the self that we should idolize it? What is there in the self that is worthy of being expressed and conveyed to others? What is the self that He be mindful of it? The self gains when absorbed in the contemplation of the non-self, in the contemplation of God, for example. Our supreme goal is *self-attachment* to what is greater than the self rather than *self-expression*.

Still, there is a tension between our insistence that prayer is an outburst of the heart, spontaneity, and the insistence that prayer must be bound to a fixed liturgy, largely confined to a particular text, to some definite words or means of expression. An authority such as Bahya Ibn Paquda reminds us: "It is meet, my brother, that thou shouldst know that our object in prayer is but the consummation of the soul's longing for God and its humiliation before Him, coupled with its exaltation of the Creator, its bestowal of praise and gratitude upon His name, and its casting of all its burdens upon Him." However, since it is difficult for the soul to recall all the thoughts that one ought to have in an act of worship, "and also because the mind is unstable, owing to the swiftness with which fancies pass through it . . . our wise men, peace be unto them, composed the Order of Prayers."[3] With these remarks we must concur.

What we said about self-expression applies to empathy. There is no such a thing as *absolute* empathy, as empathy without expression. Genuine response to the liturgical word is more than an automatic echo; it is an answer of the whole person. Empathy, moreover, is evocative; it calls up what is hidden. Every one of us bears a vast accumulation of unuttered sorrows, scruples, hopes, and yearnings, frozen in the muteness of our natures. In prayer, the ice breaks, our feelings begin to move our mind, striving for an outlet. Empathy generates expression.

On the other hand, tradition requires of us to add a silent private prayer each time we recite the fixed liturgy. Thus, over and above the pattern of the liturgy, we ought to bring to expression, or at least to our consciousness, what concerns us most at the moment.

Those who plead for the primacy of the prayer of expression over the prayer of empathy ought to remember that the ability to express what is hidden in the heart is a rare gift, and cannot be counted upon by all men. What, as a rule, makes it possible for us to pray is our ability to affiliate our own minds with the pattern of fixed texts, to unlock our hearts to the words, and to surrender to their meanings. The words stand before us as living entities full of spiritual power, of a power which often surpasses the grasp of our minds. The words are often the givers, and we the recipients. They inspire our minds and awaken our hearts.

Most of us do not know the answer to one of the most important questions, namely, What is our ultimate concern? We do not know what to pray for. It is the liturgy that teaches us

[3]Bahya Ibn Paquda, *The Duties of the Heart,* ed. by Moses Haymson, Vol. IV, p. 72.

what to pray for. It is through the words of the liturgy that we discover what moves us unawares, what is urgent in our lives, what in us is related to the ultimate.

We do not realize how much we acquire by dwelling upon the treasures of the liturgy until we learn how to commune with the spirit of Israel's prophets and saints. It is more inspiring to let the heart echo the music of the ages than to play upon the broken flutes of our own hearts. There is more promise in proceeding from above inward, from the spirit to the soul, than vice versa. Carried away on the wings of praying words, we are at once in a sphere where our thoughts may be released from the pitiful prison of the platitudes of self and be led to a sphere in which we may exchange grief for hope, thought for light. In contrast, proceeding from the subjective, from one's own inwardness, it is so hard to find a way out of the narrowness of self.

It is good that there are words sanctified by ages of worship, by the honesty and love of generations. If it were left to ourselves, who would know what word is right to be offered as praise in the sight of God or which of our perishable thoughts is worthy of entering eternity?

On the other hand, one may ask: Why should we follow the order of the liturgy? Should we not say, one ought to pray when he is ready to pray? The time to pray is all the time. There is always an opportunity to disclose the holy, but when we fail to seize it, there are definite moments in the liturgical order of the day, there are words in the liturgical order of our speech to remind us. These words are like mountain peaks pointing to the unfathomable. Ascending their trails we arrive at prayer.[4]

Prayer Is a Pilgrimage

There is danger in the prayer of empathy, the danger of relying on the word, of depending upon the text, of forgetting that the word is a challenge to the soul rather than a substitute for

4See p. 97.

the outburst of the heart. Even in prayer of empathy the word is, at best, the inspirer, not the source. The source is the soul. Prayer as a way of speaking is a way that leads nowhere. The text must never be more important than *kavanah*, than inner devotion. The life of prayer depends not so much upon loyalty to custom as upon inner participation; not so much upon the length as upon the depth of the service.

Those who run precipitately through the liturgy, rushing in and out of the prayer-texts, as if the task were to cover a maximum of space in a minimum of time, will derive little from worship. To be able to pray is to know how to stand still and to dwell upon a word. This is how some worshipers of the past would act: "They would repeat the same word many times, because they loved and cherished it so much that they could not part from it."[5]

"The worshiper must direct his heart to each and every word. He is like a man who walks in a garden collecting roses and rare flowers, plucking them one by one, in order to weave a garland. So the worshiper moves from letter to letter, from word to word, uniting them in prayer. Every word seizes hold of him and cleaves to his soul, and entreats him not to abandon it, not to break their bond, saying: *Consider my light, my grace, my splendor. Am I not the word 'Baruch' (Blessed) Hearken to me when you pronounce me. Consider me when you utter me.*"[6]

The distinguished scholar Rabbi Menahem Lonzano who lived in the sixteenth century in Safed complained about the fact that the hours which are daily devoted to worship are not sufficient to concentrate one's mind upon each passage of the liturgy. "I know for myself," he maintains, "that even though I am fluent in speech and able to speak articulately I cannot keep up with the speed of congregational service. . . . In short, people may be divided into two classes: those who [bring about harmony between God and the world], proclaiming His oneness, pray to Him and bless Him, and those who say the words of oneness but

[5]Rabbi Zevi Elimelech of Dynov, *Igra Depirka*, p. 62.
[6]Rabbi Nahman of Bratzlav, *Likkute Maharan*, Lemberg, 1876, Part I, Ch. 65, p. 80c.

do not add to the harmony between God [and the world]; they say the words of prayer but do not pray; they say the words of blessing but do not bless. Behold, I have searched and discovered that the first group is very small in number, while the second group is as numerous as the locusts. May I myself not become one of them."[7]

There is a classical principle in regard to prayer: "*Better is a little with kavanah than much without it.*"[8] Quality is more decisive than quantity. Jewish piety throughout the ages expressed itself by adding more prayers to the liturgy. The prayer book of the last centuries contains many more texts than the prayer book in the time of the Talmud or in the time of Saadia. A pilgrimage through the entire order of the daily morning prayer in its present form is like a journey through a vast collection of precious works of art. To absorb all their beauty, even to a small degree, would take many hours of concentration as well as the ability to experience an immense variety of insights, one after the other. But the time allotted to daily prayer is too brief, and all we are able to accomplish is a hasty glance.

To abridge the service without deepening the concentration would be meaningless. It is just as possible to read a brief service without *kavanah* as to go through a long service without *kavanah*. On the other hand, those of us who are anxious to omit no word out of reverence for the treasures of the liturgy are paying a high price for their loyalty. Judaism is faced with a dilemma, with a conflict between two requirements: the loyalty to the order and the requirement of *kavanah*.

Two brief stories may be told relative to the two main types of prayer, the expressive and the empathic.

There was a young shepherd who was unable to recite the Hebrew prayers. The only way in which he worshiped was "Lord of the world! It is apparent and known unto you, that if you had cattle and gave them to me to tend, though I take wages for tending from all others, from you I would take nothing, because I love you."

[7]*Derech Hayim*, Lemberg, 1931, p. 100.
[8]*Tur Orah Hayim*, Ch. 61.

35

One day a learned man passing by heard the shepherd pronounce his offer and shouted at him: "Fool, do not pray thus."

The shepherd asked him: "How should I pray?"

Thereupon the learned man taught him the benedictions in order, the recitation of the *Shema*[9] and the "silent prayer," so that henceforth he would not say what he was accustomed to say.

After the learned man had gone away, the shepherd forgot all that had been taught him, and did not pray. And he was even afraid to say what he had been accustomed to say, since the righteous man had told him not to.

One night the learned man had a dream, and in it he heard a voice: "If you do not tell him to say what he was accustomed to say before you came to him, know that misfortune will overtake you, for you have robbed me of one who belongs to the world to come."

At once the learned man went to the shepherd and said to him: "What prayer are you making?"

The shepherd answered: "None, for I have forgotten what you taught me, and you forbade me to say 'If you had cattle.'"

Then the learned man told him what he had dreamed and added: "Say what you used to say."

"Behold, here is one who had neither Torah nor words; he only had it in his heart to do good, and this was esteemed in heaven, as if this were a great thing. *The Merciful One desires the Heart.*[10] Therefore, let men think good thoughts, and let these thoughts be turned to the Holy One, blessed be he."[11]

Now, many of us are so much on the side of the shepherd-boy as to be opposed to the institution of regular prayer, claiming that one should pray when and as we feel inspired to do so. For such there is a story, told by Rabbi Israel Friedman, the Rizhiner, about a small Jewish town, far off from the main roads of the land. But it had all the necessary municipal institutions: a bath-

[9]"Hear, O Israel," core of the morning and evening prayers, consisting of the following passages: Deuteronomy 6:4–9, 11:13–21; Numbers 15:37–41.

[10]Cf. *Sanhedrin*, 106b.

[11]*Sefer Hasidim*, ed. by J. Wistinetzki, Berlin, 1891, p. 6; Nahum N. Glatzer, *In Time and Eternity*, New York, 1946, pp. 88–89.

36

house, a cemetery, a hospital, and law court; as well as all sorts of craftsmen—tailors, shoemakers, carpenters, and masons. One trade, however, was lacking: there was no watchmaker. In the course of years many of the clocks became so annoyingly inaccurate that their owners just decided to let them run down, and ignore them altogether. There were others, however, who maintained that as long as the clocks ran, they should not be abandoned. So they wound their clocks day after day though they knew that they were not accurate. One day the news spread through the town that a watchmaker had arrived, and everyone rushed to him with their clocks. But the only ones he could repair were those that had been kept running—the abandoned clocks had grown too rusty!

Prayer Begins Where Expression Ends

Prayer, as we shall see, is dominated by a polarity of regularity and sponetaneity, of the stillness of a fixed text (*keva*) and of the motivity of inner devotion (*kavanah*), of empathy and self-expression. The ambivalence of the word is another example of the polarity. From the point of view of empathy, of *keva*, the word stands for more than the mind can absorb; from the point of view of self-expression, of *kavanah*, the mind bears more than the word can convey. For, as said above, just as there are words that lie beyond our power of empathy, there are thoughts that lie beyond our power of expression.

Prayer, we are told, "consists of words and thoughts. Words are in need of thoughts, yet thoughts are not in need of speech": they may be composed within the heart. The thoughts are the essence of devotion, not the words. "The thought of prayer requires no words in a situation where it is possible to compose it entirely in the heart. And it is the thought that is the essence

37

of our devotion, and is the stay upon which our object in prayer must rest."[12]

The role of the word is in a sense comparable to the role of the synagogue. "The Holy One said to the community of Israel —I have instructed you to pray in the synagogues of your cities. But if you are unable to pray in the synagogues, you may pray in your homes. If you are unable to pray in your homes, you may pray in your beds. If you are unable to pray in your beds, then meditate in your hearts. For this is the meaning of the verse in Psalms (4:5): *Commune with your heart . . . and be still.*"[13]

"A man who has been granted knowledge and given understanding will be sensitive to the special wisdom with which God phrased the commandment concerning prayer. He has not just written 'pray to me' or 'beseech me' or 'ask of me and I will answer.' When he commanded us to study Torah it was enough to say 'Thou shalt speak of them' or 'Thou shalt teach them unto thy children.' But when He came to give the commandment of prayer, He said something more: '*to serve Him with all your heart*' (Deuteronomy 11:13). Prayer was a commandment given to the heart and it can be fulfilled only by the heart. Therefore, he who brings God the offering of his heart fulfills the commandment; he who brings Him only words does not.

"And if it were somehow possible to worship without words; if the heart could be offered alone; this would be enough to fulfill the commandment."[14]

In the early days, we are told, the appearance of the new moon—which meant the advent of a new month—was announced all over Palestine by the lighting of *torches*. It was after the heretics began to confuse the people by creating false signals through lighting torches at the wrong times, that *messengers* had

[12]Bahya Ibn Paquda, *The Duties of the Heart*, ed. Haymson, Vol. IV, p. 72. In support of his view, Bahya quotes the Rabbinic rule that "in the time of emergency, he who is ritually unclean may meditate his prayer in his heart, and need not say the necessary benedictions, neither before nor after it." Another evidence is the fact that in certain situations the law permits one to condense the regular form of prayer.

[13]*Midrash Tehillim*, ed. by Buber, 4, 9.

[14]Rabbi Menahem Lonzano, *Derech Hayim*, p. 84.

to be sent to every community instead of lighting torches.[15]

This has been interpreted in the following way: In early times when the hearts of men burned with love for the Creator, when their desire to serve Him overflowed all limits, it was not necessary to verbalize the act of prayer; they did not have to bring it *from the heart to the lips.*

But since the time that heresies have divided the hearts of men, they had to institute the sending of messengers. In order to protect and express the desires of the heart, they were forced to use words, instruments. This is how speech came to be the vehicle of prayer.[16]

In a sense, prayer begins where expression ends. The words that reach our lips are often but waves of an overflowing stream touching the shore. We often seek and miss, struggle and fail to adjust our unique feelings to the patterns of texts. The soul can only intimate its persistent striving, the riddle of its unhappiness, the strain of living twixt hope and fear. Where is the tree that can utter fully the silent passion of the soil? Words can only open the door, and we can only weep on the threshold of our incommunicable thirst after the incomprehensible.

In no other act does man experience so often the disparity between the desire for expression and the means of expression as in prayer. The inadequacy of the means at our disposal appears so tangible, so tragic, that one feels it a grace to be able to give oneself up to music, to a tone, to a song, to a chant. The wave of a song carries the soul to heights which utterable meanings can never reach. Such abandonment is no escape nor an act of being unfaithful to the mind. For the world of unutterable meanings is the nursery of the soul, the cradle of all our ideas. It is not an escape but a return to one's origins.

What the word can no longer yield, man achieves through the fullness of his powerlessness. The deeper the need in which one

[15]*Mishnah Rosh Hashanah* 11, 1.
[16]Rabbi Nota of Avrutsh, quoted by Rabbi David Shomo of Tultshin, *Hitoreruth Hatefillah*, Pietrkow, 1911, p. 17. Theoretically Maimonides seems to prefer extemporaneous unfixed prayer, and sees the reason for the institution of fixed prayer in the linguistic confusion of the people which set in since the time of the exile. *Mishne Torah*, Tefillah, 1, 3.

is placed through this powerlessness, the more does man reveal himself in his essence, and himself becomes expression. Prayer is more than communication, and man is more than the word.

Should we feel ashamed of our inability to utter what we bear in our hearts? A certain passage in the morning liturgy was interpreted by Rabbi Wolf of Zhitomir to mean that God loves what is left over at the bottom of the heart and cannot be expressed in words.[17] It is the ineffable in us which reaches God rather than the expressed feeling. The unutterable surplus of what we feel, the sentiments that we are unable to put into words are our payment in kind to God.

We read in the Psalms (5:2):

> *Give ear to my words, O Lord,*
> *Understand my insight.*

According to the Midrash, David said: "Lord of the world, at a time when I have strength to stand before Thee in prayer, and to bring forth words—give ear! At a time when I have no strength to bring forth words—understand what is in my heart, *understand my faltering*."[18]

"A man stands at prayer and meditates in his heart [without uttering a word], and God is near unto his prayer . . . David said, *Answer me when I call* (Psalms 4:2). Said God to him, *'You say, Answer me when I call;* by your life, even before you call will I answer you,' as it is said, *Before they call I will answer* (Isaiah 65:24)."[19]

God hears not only prayer but also the desire to pray. "The desire and intention of the pure and upright are fulfilled even when not expressed, as it is written: *He fulfills the desire of all who fear him* (Psalms 145:19).[20]

[17]The text reads *beshire zymrah*. Rabbi Wolf explained it as if it were vocalized *besheyare*. Rabbi Phinehas of Turka, *Heshev Haephod*, Lemberg, 1862, p. 226.

[18]*Midrash Tehillim*, 5, 6.

[19]*Deuteronomy Rabba*, 2, 10.

[20]Rabbi Moses ben Joseph di Trani (1505–1585), *Bet Elohim*, Venice, 1576, p. 6b.

40

"To Thee Silence Is Praise"

The sense for the power of words and the sense for the impotence of human expression are equally characteristic of the religious consciousness. "Who can utter the mighty doings of the Lord or utter all his praise?" (Psalms 106:2). He is "exalted above all blessing and praise" (Nehemiah 9:5), "above all the blessings and hymns, extollings and comfortings that are ever uttered in the world" (the *kaddish*). This is the most important guidance:

> *Commune with your hearts . . .*
> *and be still.*
>
> Psalms 4:5

"The highest form of worship is that of silence and hope."[21] "The language of the heart is the main thing; the spoken word serves merely as an interpreter between the heart and the listener."[22] "The preparations of the heart are man's, but the expression (or answer) of the tongue is from the Lord" (Proverbs 16:1). "*For there is a form of knowledge that precedes the process of expression* (compare Psalms 139:4), and it is God who understands it."[23]

We read in the second book of Kings 4:8 that Elisha the prophet as often as he came to the town of Shunem would eat bread in the house of a wealthy woman. And she said to her husband: Behold now, I perceive that this is a holy man of God. Let us make a special chamber for him. In the Talmud the question is discussed how did she recognize that he was a holy man? An answer given is that she noticed a sign of sanctity. To Rabbi Nahman of Kobryn, this discussion seemed strange. Why was there the need of a sign? Is it so difficult to recognize a holy man?

[21]Ibn Gabirol, *The Choice of Pearls*, ed. Ascher, 66.
[22]Ibn Ezra, *Commentary on Psalms*, 4:5.
[23]Ibn Ezra, *Commentary on Proverbs*, 16:1.

This is how he explained the Talmudic passage. There are four levels of piety, and each has its own nature of worshipping God. We read in the Sabbath liturgy (in the Ashkenazic version):

By the mouth of the upright Thou art praised;
By the words of the righteous Thou art blessed;
By the tongue of the faithful Thou art extolled,
And within the holy Thou art sanctified.

Those who reach the lowest stage of piety are called the upright; their worship is expressed through the mouth. Higher than these are the righteous; their worship is not expressed through the mouth but in the mere movement of the lips. Higher than these are the faithful; their worship is on the tongue; it does not even pass the lips. The highest kind is the holy men; their worship is hidden and concealed within them and is apparent only to Him who knows all secrets. This is why the Talmud asked: How did she recognize that he was a holy man? For if he is holy, then his holiness is hidden. This is why the woman of Shunem needed a sign that Elisha was a holy man.

Arriving at his highest understanding, man is reduced to stillness.

To Thee silence is praise.
Psalms 65:2[24]

The Lord is in his holy temple;
Let all the earth keep silence
before him.
Habakkuk 2:20

Be silent before the Lord God . . .
Be silent, all flesh, before the Lord.
Zephaniah 1:7
Zechariah 2:13

For there is not a word in my tongue,
But, lo, O Lord, thou knowest it all.
Psalms 139:4

[24]The verb means "to be silent," see Rashi and Targum. Compare also Psalms 62:2 and the Targum.

One must never forget the ancient maxim, "the best medicament is silence. The more you praise a flawless pearl, the more you depreciate it."[25] "He who is wisest in the knowledge of God knows that he is most ignorant of this essence; while he who does not know Him, claims to know His essence."[26] It is the awareness of the paradox that gives the right to utter his praise.

> *I tell Thy praise, though I have not seen Thee,*
> *I describe Thee, though I have not known Thee.*
> The Song of Unity

"A certain reader once prayed in the presence of Rabbi Hanina and said: 'O God, the great, the mighty, the revered, the majestic, the powerful, the strong, the fearless, the all-wise, the certain, the honorable," etc., etc. Rabbi Hanina waited until he finished and then said to him: 'Have you exhausted the praises of your Master? Why do you say so much? Even the three attributes which we recite (in "The silent prayer": great, mighty, revered), we do so only because our master Moses put them in his law and because the men of the Great Assembly fixed them in the liturgy. It is as if an earthly king had a million denarii of gold, and we praised him for possessing much silver. Is not such praise insult?' "[27]

"One who descants upon the praises of the Holy One, blessed be He, to excess is uprooted from the world. *Shall it be told Him that I speak? If a man speak, surely he shall be swallowed up* (Job 37:20). . . . *For to Thee silence is praise* (Psalms 65:2). The best medicament of all is silence."[28]

Only he can praise Him who is profoundly aware of his ability to praise Him.

> *Were our mouth filled with song as the sea is*
> *with water,*

[25]*Megillah* 18a; *Jerushalmi Megillah IX,* beginning; *Midrash Tehillim,* Ch. 19, 2.
[26]Bahya, *The Duties of the Heart,* I, 10.
[27]*Berachot* 33b.
[28]*Megillah* 18a.

and our tongue with ringing praise as the
roaring waves;
were our lips full of adoration as the wide
expanse of heaven,
and our eyes sparkling like the sun or the moon;
were our hands spread out in prayer as the eagles
of the sky
and our feet as swift as the deer . . .
we should still be unable to thank thee and to
bless thy name.[29]

In a sense, our liturgy is a higher form of silence. It is pervaded by an awed sense of the grandeur of God which resists description and surpasses all expression. The individual is silent. He does not bring forth his own words. His saying the consecrated words is in essence an act of listening to what they convey. *The spirit of Israel speaks, the self is silent.*

Twofold is the meaning of silence. One, the abstinence from speech, the absence of sound. Two, inner silence, the absence of self-concern, stillness. One may articulate words in his voice and yet be inwardly silent. One may abstain from uttering any sound and yet be overbearing.

Both are inadequate: our speech as well as our silence. Yet there is a level that goes beyond both: the level of song. "There are three ways in which a man expresses his deep sorrow: the man on the lowest level cries; the man on the second level is silent; the man on the highest level knows how to turn his sorrow into song."[30] True prayer is a song.

Prayer and the Community

We have stressed the fact that prayer is an event that begins

[29]From The Sabbath Liturgy, *The Daily Prayer Book*, ed. by Philip Birnbaum, p. 331.
[30]*Seah Sarfe Kodesh*, vol. 2, p. 92, §318.

in the individual soul. We have not dwelled upon how much our ability to pray depends upon our being a part of a community of prayer.

It is not safe to pray alone. Tradition insists that we pray with, and as a part of, the community; that public worship is preferable to private worship. Here we are faced with an aspect of the *polarity of prayer*. There is a permanent union between individual worship and community worship, each of which depends for its existence upon the other. To ignore their *spiritual symbiosis* will prove fatal to both.

How can we forget that our ability to pray we owe to the community and to tradition? We have learned how to pray by listening to the voice of prayer, by having been a part of a community of men standing before God. We are often carried toward prayer by the reader: when we hear how he asks questions, how he implores, cries, humbles himself, sings.

Those who cherish genuine prayer, yet feel driven away from the houses of worship because of the sterility of public worship today, seem to believe that private prayer is the only way. Yet, the truth is that private prayer will not survive unless it is inspired by public prayer. The way of the recluse, the exclusive concern with personal salvation, piety in isolation from the community is an act of impiety.

Judaism is not only the adherence to particular doctrines and observances, but primarily living in the spiritual order of the Jewish people, the living *in* the Jews of the past and *with* the Jews of the present. Judaism is not only a certain quality in the souls of the individuals, but primarily the existence of the community of Israel. It is not a doctrine, an idea, a faith, but the covenant between God and the people. Our share in holiness we acquire by living in the Jewish community. What we do as individuals is a trivial episode; what we attain as Israel causes us to become a part of eternity.

The Jew does not stand alone before God; it is as a member of the community that he stands before God. Our relationship to Him is not as an I to a Thou, but as a We to a Thou.[31]

31See p. 55.

We never pray as individuals, set apart from the rest of the world. The liturgy is an order which we can enter only as a part of the Community of Israel. Every act of worship is an act of participating in an eternal service, in the service of all souls of all ages. Every act of adoration is done in union with all of history, and with all beings above and below:

> *We sanctify Thy Name in the world, as they sanctify*
> *it in the highest heavens . . .*
> *A crown will be bestowed*
> *Upon the Lord our God*
> *By the angels, the multitudes above,*
> *In union with Israel Thy people*
> *Assembled below. . . .*[32]

And yet—this we must never forget—prayer is primarily an event in the individual souls, an act of emanation, not only an act of participation. Even the worth of public worship depends upon the depth of private worship, of the private worship of those who worship together. We are taught that the fate of all mankind depends upon the conduct of one single individual, namely you.[33] This undoubtedly applies to what goes on in the houses of worship.

The tragedy is that public worship in our time seems to have gone in a direction where genuine prayer is hardly encouraged. Let us attempt to offer an analysis of the contemporary situation.

[32]The *kaddish* in the liturgy for the Sabbath morning.
[33]*Kiddushin*, 40b.

3

Spontaneity Is
the Goal

Praying by Proxy

Services are conducted with dignity and precision. The rendition of the liturgy is smooth. Everything is present: decorum, voice, ceremony. But one thing is missing: *Life*. One knows in advance what will ensue. There will be no surprise, no adventure of the soul; there will be no sudden outburst of devotion. Nothing is going to happen to the soul. Nothing unpredictable must happen to the person who prays. He will attain no insight into the words he reads; he will attain no new perspective for the life he lives. Our motto is monotony. The fire has gone out of our worship. It is cold, stiff, and dead. True, things are happening;

of course, not within prayer, but within the administration of the temples. Do we not establish new edifices all over the country?

Yes, the edifices are growing. Yet, worship is decaying.

Has the temple become the graveyard where prayer is buried? There are many who labor in the vineyard of oratory; but who knows how to pray, or how to inspire others to pray? There are many who can execute and display magnificent fireworks; but who knows how to kindle a spark in the darkness of a soul?

Of course, people still attend "services"—but what does this attendance frequently mean to them? Outpouring of the soul? Worship? Prayer, temple attendance has become a service of the community rather than service of God. People give some of their money to philanthropic causes, and some of their time to the temple.

The modern temple suffers from *a severe cold*. Congregants preserve a respectful distance between the liturgy and themselves. They say the words, "Forgive us for we have sinned," but of course, they are not meant. They say, "Thou shalt love the Lord Thy God with all thy heart . . ." in lofty detachment, in complete anonymity as if giving an impartial opinion about an irrelevant question.

An air of tranquillity, complacency prevails in our houses of worship. What can come out of such an atmosphere? The services are prim, the voice is dry, the temple is clean and tidy, and the soul of prayer lies in agony. You know no one will scream, no one will cry, the words will be still-born.

People expect the rabbi to conduct a service: an efficient, expert service. But efficiency and rapidity are no remedy against devotional sterility.

We have developed the habit of *praying by proxy*. Many congregants seem to have adopted the principle of vicarious prayer. The rabbi or the cantor does the praying for the congregation. Men and women would not raise their voices, unless the rabbi issues the signal. Alas, they have come to regard the rabbi as a master of ceremonies.

Is not their mood, in part, a reflection of our own uncertainties? Prayer has become an empty gesture, a figure of speech.

50

Either because of lack of faith or because of *religious bashful- ness*. We would not admit that we take prayer seriously. It would sound sanctimonious, if not hypocritical. We are too sophisti- cated. But if prayer is as important as study, if prayer is as precious a deed as an act of charity, we must stop being em- barrassed at our saying *Praised be Thou* with inner devotion.

Ours is a great responsibility. We demand that people come to worship instead of playing golf, or making money, or going on a picnic. Why? Don't we mislead them? People take their precious time off to attend services. Some even arrive with pro- found expectations. But what do they get? What do they receive?

Spiritual Absenteeism

There is another privation: the loss of *grace*. Our services have so little charm, so little grace. What is grace? The presence of the soul. A person has grace when the throbbing of his heart is audible in his voice; when the longings of his soul animate his face. Now, how do our people pray? They recite the prayer book as if it were last week's newspaper. They ensconce in anonymity —as if prayer were an impersonal exercise—as if worship were an act that came automatically. The words are there but the souls who are to feel their meaning, to absorb their significance, are absent. They utter shells of syllables, but put nothing of them- selves into the shells. In our daily speech, in uttering a sentence, our words have a tonal quality. There is no communication with- out intonation. It is the intonation that indicates what we mean by what we say, so that we can discern whether we hear a ques- tion, an exclamation, or an assertion.

It is the *intonation* that lends grace to what we say. But when we pray, the words faint on our lips. Our words have no tone, no strength, no personal dimension, as if we did not mean what we said; as if reading paragraphs in Roget's *Thesaurus*. It is prayer without grace. Of course, they are offered plenty of re- sponsive reading, but there is little responsiveness to what they read. No one knows how to shed a tear. No one is ready to invest a sigh. Is there no tear in their souls?

> *Is there no balm in Gilead?*
> *Is there no physician there?*
> *Why then is not the health*
> *Of the daughter of my people recovered?*

Assembled in the synagogue everything is there—the body, the benches, the books. But one thing is absent: soul. It is as if we all suffered from *spiritual absenteeism.* In good prayer, words become one with the soul. Yet in our synagogues, people who are otherwise sensitive, vibrant, arresting, sit there aloof, listless, lazy. *The dead praise not the Lord* (Psalms 115:17). Those who are spiritually dull cannot praise God.

That we sensed that this is a problem is evidenced by the many valiant but futile attempts to deal with it. The problem, namely, of how to increase synagogue attendance. A variety of suggestions have been made, e.g., to bring the liturgy up to date by composing shorter and better prayers; to invite distinguished speakers, radio-commentators and columnists, to arrange congregational forums, panels and symposia; to celebrate annual projects such as "Jewish Culture Sabbath," "Jewish War Veterans Sabbath," "Boy Scouts Sabbath," "Interfaith Sabbath" (why not a "*Sabbath* Sabbath"?); to install stained glass windows; to place gold, silver or blue pledge-cards on the seats on which people would pledge regular attendance; to remind people of their birthday dates. Well-intentioned as these suggestions may be, they do not deal with the core of the issue. *Spiritual problems cannot be solved by administrative techniques.*

The problem is not how to fill the buildings but how to inspire the hearts. And this is a problem to which techniques of commercial psychology can hardly be applied. The problem is not one of *synagogue attendance* but one of *spiritual attendance.* The problem is not *how to attract bodies to enter the space of a temple* but *how to inspire souls to enter an hour of spiritual concentration in the presence of God.* The problem is *time*, not space.[1]

[1]See A. J. Heschel, *The Sabbath, Its Meaning to Modern Man*, New York, 1951, p. 8.

52

Prayer is an extremely intricate phenomenon. Numerous attempts have been made to define and to explain it. I will briefly mention four of the prevalent doctrines.

Jan. 2/88

(1) The Doctrine of Agnosticism

The doctrine of Agnosticism claims that prayer is rooted in superstition. It is "one of humanity's greatest mistakes," "a desperate effort of bewildered creatures to come to terms with surrounding mystery." Thus, prayer is a fraud. To the worshiping man we must say: "Fool, why do you in vain beseech with childish prayers, things which no day ever did bring, will bring, or could bring?"[2]

Since it is dangerous fraud, the synagogue must be abolished. A vast number of people have, indeed, eliminated prayer from their lives. They made an end to that illusion.

There are some people who believe that the only way to revitalize the synagogue is to minimize the importance of prayer and to convert the synagogue into a social center.[3] Let us face the situation. This is the law of life. Just as man cannot live without a soul, religion cannot survive without God. Our soul withers without prayer. A synagogue in which men no longer aspire to prayer is not a compromise but a defeat; a perversion, not a concession. To pray with *kavanah* (inner devotion) may be difficult; to pray without it is ludicrous.

(2) The Doctrine of Religious Behaviorism

There are people who seem to believe that religious deeds can be performed in a spiritual wasteland, in the absence of the soul, with a heart hermetically sealed; that external action is the

[2]Ovid, *Tristia*, III, 8.11.
[3]See *Shabbath*, 31b.

essential mode of worship, pedantry the same as piety; as if all that mattered is how men behaved in physical terms; as if religion were not concerned with the inner life.[4]

Such a conception, which we would like to call *religious behaviorism,* unwittingly reduces Judaism to a sort of sacred physics, with no sense for the imponderable, the introspective, the metaphysical.

As a personal attitude religious behaviorism usually reflects a widely held theology in which the supreme article of faith is *respect for tradition.* People are urged to observe the rituals or to attend services out of deference to what has come down to us from our ancestors. The *theology of respect* pleads for the maintenance of the inherited and transmitted customs and institutions and is characterized by a spirit of conformity, excessive moderation and disrespect of spontaneity. The outlook of religious behaviorists comes close to the view embodied in Seneca's saying *tamquam legibus iussa non tamquam dis grata* (observe religious customs because they are commanded by law, not because they are desired by the gods).

Wise, important, essential and pedagogically useful as the principle "respect for tradition" is, it is grotesque and self-defeating to make of it the supreme article of faith.

Religious behaviorism is a doctrine that dominates many minds, and is to a large measure responsible for the crisis of prayer.

(3) The Doctrine of Prayer as a Social Act

There is another definition which is being perpetuated all over the country in sermons, synagogue bulletins and books. *"Prayer is the identification of the worshiper with the people of Israel,"* or "the occasion for immersing ourselves in the living reality" of our people. In inviting people to join a synagogue, the idea is advanced that "The synagogue is the instrument through which

[4]On the radical importance of doing, see p. 110.

the Jew is identified with his people. The sense of identification is achieved only through common worship." Such an approach is built on a theology which regards God as a symbol of social action, as an epitome of the ideals of the group, as "the spirit of the beloved community";[5] as "the spirit of a people, and insofar as there is a world of humanity . . . the Spirit of the World";[6] as the "Creative Good Will" which makes cooperation in our moral endeavor possible.[7]

"An act of identification with the people" is, phenomenologically speaking, the definition of a political act. But is a political phenomenon the same as worship? Moreover, is the act of identification with the Jewish people in itself an act that constitutes the essence of worship? Who is our model: Elijah who disassociated himself from the congregations of his people, or the prophets of the Baal who led and identified themselves with their people? The prophets of Israel were not eager to be in agreement with popular sentiments. Spiritually important, essential, and sacred as the identification with the people Israel is, we must not forget that what lends spiritual importance and sanctity to that identification is Israel's unique association with the will of God. It is this association that raises our attachment to the people Israel above the level of mere nationalism.

The doctrine of prayer as a social act is the product of what may be called *"the sociological fallacy,"* according to which the individual has no reality except as a carrier of ideas and attitudes that are derived from group existence. Applied to Jewish faith, it is a total misunderstanding of the nature of Jewish faith to overemphasize the social or communal aspect. It is true that a Jew never worships as an isolated individual but *as a part of the Community of Israel.* Yet it is within the heart of every individual that prayer takes place. It is a personal duty, and an intimate act which cannot be delegated to either the cantor or to the whole community. We pray with all of Israel, and everyone of us by himself. Contrary to sociological theories, individual

[5] J. Royce, *The Problem of Christianity,* 1913, 1, pp. 172, 408f.
[6] E. S. Ames, *Religion,* 1929, p. 132.
[7] E. W. Lyman, *The Meaning and Truth of Religion,* 1933, p. 33.

prayer preceded collective prayer in the history of religion.

Such sociological perspectives forfeit the unique aspects of worship. Do we, in the moment of prayer, concentrate on the group? We read Psalms 63:2–5:

> O God, Thou art my God, earnestly will I seek Thee;
> My soul thirsts for Thee, my flesh faints for Thee,
> In a dry and weary land, where no water is.
> So have I looked for Thee in the sanctuary,
> To see Thy power and Thy glory.
> For Thy lovingkindness is better than life;
> My lips shall praise Thee.
> So will I bless Thee as long as I live;
> I will lift up my hands and call on Thy name.

Can the sociological definition of prayer as an act of identification with the group be applied to this Psalm?

(4) The Doctrine of Religious Solipsism

The doctrine maintains that the individual self of the worshiper is the whole sphere of prayer-life. The assumption is that God is an idea, a process, a source, a fountain, a spring, a power. But one cannot worship an idea; one cannot address his prayers to a fountain of values; one cannot pray to "whom it may concern." To whom, then, do we direct our prayers? Yes, there is an answer. As a recent writer put it: We address "prayers to the good within ourselves."[8]

I do not wish to minimize the fact that we all suffer from an ego-centric predicament. Our soul tends to confine itself to its own ideas, interests, and emotions. But why should we raise the ego-centric affliction to the status of a virtue? It is precisely the

[8]A discussion of this view, which is so popular today, is found in I. Segond, *La prière, étude de psychologie religieuse,* Paris, 1911, p. 52. It is a definition of prayer that fits into pantheism. If the deity is equated with the universe, and we ourselves are a part of the universe or the deity, then in praying to the deity, we are in essence praying to ourselves.

function of prayer to overcome that predicament, to see the world in a different setting. The self is not the hub but the spoke of the revolving wheel. It is precisely the function of prayer to shift the center of living from self-consciousness to self-surrender.[9]

Religious solipsism claims that we must continue to recite our prayers, for prayer is a useful activity. The ideas may be false; it is absurd to believe that God "hearkens to prayers and supplications," but we should say all this because it is good for one's health. Is it really good for one's health? How could intellectual dishonesty be good for the soul?

The Separation of Church and God

We are descendants of those who taught the world what true worship is. Our fathers created the only universal language there is: the language of prayer. All men in the Western world speak to God in the language of our prayers, of our Psalms. Is it not proper to ask our fathers: What is the spirit of Jewish prayer? But are we ready to ask the question? Are we qualified to understand the answer? The difficulty of our situation lies in the fact that we have inherited physical features of our fathers but failed to acquire some of their spiritual qualities. Biologically we are Jews; theologically we are pagan to a considerable degree. Our hands are the hands of Jacob, but our voice is often the voice of Esau.

There are bitter problems which religion has to solve: agony, sin, despair. There is darkness in the world. There is horror in the soul. What has the community of Israel to say to the world?

We worry a great deal about the problem of church and state. Now what about the church and God? Sometimes there seems to be a greater separation between the church and God than between the church and state.

It has become a habit with modern movements to decapitate Biblical verses. Some such decapitated verses have become famous

[9]See above, pp. 7, 15.

slogans. The name of the *Bilu* movement[10] is an abbrevation of *O house of Jacob, come ye, and let us walk* (Isaiah 2:5); the essence of the verse, *in the light of the Lord,* was omitted. Disciples of Ahad Ha'am[11] proclaimed *Not by might, nor by power, but by spirit* (Zechariah 4:6). Yet the prophet said *by My spirit.* The Jewish National Fund has as its official motto *The land shall not be sold for ever* (Leviticus 25:23); the end, *for the land is Mine,* was omitted. During the last war the popular slogan among Russian Jews was *I shall not die, but live* (Psalms 118:17); the continuation, *and declare the deeds of the Lord,* was dropped.

Prayer is the microcosm of the soul. It is the whole soul in one moment; the quintessence of all our acts; the climax of all our thoughts. It rises as high as our thoughts. Now, if the Torah is nothing but the national literature of the Jewish people; if the mystery of revelation is discarded as superstition, then prayer is hardly more than a soliloquy. If God does not have power to speak to us, how should we possess the power to speak to Him? Thus, prayer is a part of a greater issue. It depends upon the total spiritual situation of man and upon a mind within which God is at home. Of course, if our lives are too barren to bring forth the spirit of worship; if all our thoughts and anxieties do not contain enough spiritual substance to be distilled into prayer, an inner transformation is a matter of emergency. And such an emergency we face today. *The issue of prayer is not prayer; the issue of prayer is God.* One cannot pray unless he has faith in his own ability to accost the infinite, merciful, eternal God.

Moreover, we must not overlook one of the profound principles of Judaism. There is something which is far greater than my desire to pray, namely, God's desire that I pray. There is something which is far greater than my will to believe, namely, God's will that I believe. How insignificant is the outpouring of my soul in the midst of this great universe! Unless it is the will of God that I pray, unless God desires our prayer,[12] how ludicrous is all my praying.

[10]A group of dedicated students who migrated from Russia to Palestine in 1882.

[11]The pen-name of Asher Ginzberg, an influential thinker (1856–1927).

[12]See *Exodus Rabba*, 21, 5; *Midrash Tehillim*, 5, 7.

58

We cannot reach heaven by building a Tower of Babel. The Biblical way *to* God is a way *of* God. God's waiting for our prayer is that which lends meaning to them.

How should we define prayer? Since it is, first of all, a phenomenon of the human consciousness, we must ask: What is it that a person is conscious of in a moment of prayer? There is a classical statement in rabbinic literature that expresses the spiritual minimum of prayer as an act of the consciousness of man: *"Know before Whom you stand."*[13] Three ideas are contained in this definition.[14]

Know (or Understand)

A certain understanding or awareness, a definite attitude of the mind is the condition *sine qua non* of all prayer. Prayer cannot live in a theological vacuum. *It comes out of insight.*

Prayer must not be treated as if it were the result of an intellectual oversight, as if it thrived best in the climate of thoughtlessness. One needs understanding, wisdom of the spirit to know what it means to worship God. Or at least one must endeavor to become free of the folly of worshiping the specious glory of mind-made deities, free of unconditional attachment to the false dogmas that populate our minds.

To live without prayer is to live without God, to live without a soul. No one is able to think of Him unless he has learned how to pray to Him. For this is the way man learns to think of the true God—of the God of Israel. He first is aware of His presence long before he thinks of His essence. And to pray is to sense His presence.

[13]*Berachoth* 28b; *Aboth de Rabbi Nathan,* Version B., Ch. 19; *Orhot Hayim,* 18.

[14]The sentence consists of three parts: The main verb in the imperative "know." Dependent on this main verb is the clause "before whom you stand" which can be broken up into two segments, the adverbial phrase "before whom" which contains the interrogative pronoun and "you stand" which is the subject and verb of the subordinate clause.

There are people who maintain that prayer is a matter of *emotion*. In their desire to "revitalize" prayer, they would proclaim: Let there be emotion! This is, of course, based on a fallacy. Emotion is an important *component;* it is not the *source* of prayer. The power to pray does not depend on whether a person is of a choleric or phlegmatic temperament. One may be extremely emotional and be unable to generate that power. This is decisive: worship comes out of insight. It is not the result of an intellectual oversight.

What is more, prayer has the power to generate insight; it often endows us with an understanding not attainable by speculation. Some of our deepest insights, decisions and attitudes are born in moments of prayer. Often where reflection fails, prayer succeeds. What thinking is to philosophy, prayer is to religion. And prayer can go beyond speculation. The truth of holiness is not a truth of speculation—it is the truth of worship.

"Rabbi said: I am amazed that the prayer for understanding was not included in the Sabbath liturgy! For if there is no understanding, how is it possible to pray?"[15]

Know before Whom you stand. Such knowledge, such understanding is not easily won. It "is neither a gift we receive undeservedly nor a treasure to be found inadvertently." The art of awareness of God, the art of sensing His presence in our daily lives, cannot be learned off-hand. "God's grace resounds in our lives like a staccato. Only by retaining the seemingly disconnected notes comes the ability to grasp the theme."[16]

That understanding we no longer try to acquire. In the modern seminaries for the training of rabbis and teachers the art of understanding what prayer implies was not a part of the curriculum. And so it is not the Psalmist, Rabbi Jehudah Halevi, Rabbi Isaiah Horovitz or Rabbi Nahman of Bratslav; it is Hegel, Freud, or Dewey who have become our guides in matters of Jewish prayer and God.

[15]*Jerushalm: Berachoth* 4, 4, 8b.
[16]A. J. Heschel, *Man Is Not Alone,* p. 88.

Before Whom

To have said before *what* would have contradicted the spirit of Jewish prayer. *What* is the most indefinite pronoun. In asking *what*, one is totally uncommitted, uninitiated, bare of any anticipation of an answer; any answer may be acceptable. But he who is totally uncommitted, who does not even have an inkling of the answer, has not learned the meaning of the ultimate question, and is not ready to engage in prayer.[17] If God is a *what*, a power, the sum total of values, how can we pray to it? An "I" does not pray to an "it." Unless, therefore, God is at least as real as my own self; unless I am sure that God has at least as much life as I do, how can I pray?

You Stand

The act of prayer is more than a process of the mind and a movement of the lips. It is an act that happens between man and God—in the presence of God.

Reading or studying the text of a prayer is not the same as praying. What marks the act of prayer is the decision to enter and face the presence of God. To pray means to expose oneself to Him, to His judgment.

If "prayer is the expression of the sense of being at home in the universe,"[18] then the Psalmist who exclaimed, "I am a stranger on earth, hide not Thy commandments from me" (119:19), was a person who grievously misunderstood the nature of prayer. Throughout many centuries of Jewish history the true motivation for prayer was not "the sense of being at home in the uni-

[17]A. J. Heschel, *ibidem*, Ch. 8 (The Ultimate Question).
[18]E. S. Ames, *Religion*, p. 217.

61

verse" but the sense of *not* being at home in the universe. We could not but experience anxiety and spiritual homelessness in the sight of so much suffering and evil, in the countless examples of failure to live up to the will of God. That experience gained in intensity by the soul-stirring awareness that God Himself was not at home in a universe, where His will is defied, where His kingship is denied. *The Shechinah is in exile,* the world is corrupt, *the universe itself is not at home. . . .*

To pray, then, means to bring God back into the world, to establish His kingship, to let His glory prevail. This is why in the greatest moments of our lives, on the Days of Awe, we cry out of the depth of our disconcerted souls, a prayer of redemption:

And so, Lord our God, grant Thy awe to all Thy works, and your dread to all Thou hast created, that all Thy works may fear Thee, and all who have been created prostrate themselves before Thee, and all form one union to do Thy will with a whole heart.

Great is the power of prayer. For to worship is to expand the presence of God in the world. God is transcendent, but our worship makes Him immanent. This is implied in the idea that God is in need of man: His being immanent depends upon us.[19] When we say *Blessed be He,* we extend His glory, we bestow His spirit upon this world. *Yithgadal Ve-yithkadash: Magnified and sanctified be God's great name throughout the world. . . .* May there be more of God in this world.

What is decisive is not the mystic experience of our being close to Him; decisive is not our *feeling* but our *certainty* of His being close to us—although even His presence is veiled and beyond the scope of our emotion. Decisive is not our emotion but our *conviction.* If such conviction is lacking, if the presence of God is a myth, then prayer to God is a delusion. If God is unable to listen to us, then we are insane in talking to Him.

The true source of prayer, we said above, is not an emotion but an insight. It is the insight into the mystery of reality, *the sense of the ineffable,* that enables us to pray. As long as we refuse to take notice of what is beyond our sight, beyond our

[19] A. J. Heschel, *Man Is Not Alone,* Ch. 23.

reason; as long as we are blind to the mystery of being, the way to prayer is closed to us. If the rise of the sun is but a daily routine of nature, there is no reason to say, *In mercy Thou givest light to the earth and to those who dwell on it . . . every day constantly.* If bread is nothing but flour moistened, kneaded, baked and then brought forth from the oven, it is meaningless to say, *Blessed art Thou . . . who bringest forth bread from the earth.*

The way to prayer leads through *acts of wonder* and *radical amazement.* The illusion of total intelligibility, the indifference to the mystery that is everywhere, the foolishness of ultimate self-reliance are serious obstacles on the way. It is in moments of our being faced with the mystery of living and dying, of knowing and not-knowing, of love and the inability of love—that we pray, that *we address ourselves to Him who is beyond the mystery.*

"Why do the sages say that a person who raises his voice during prayer is of little faith? Because prayer implies that we believe in God's willingness to answer man's petitions. Faith, believing in God, is attachment to the highest realm, the realm of the mystery. This is its essence. Our faith is capable of reaching the realm of the mystery. Perhaps this is why the word for faith (*amen, amanah, emunah*) begins with the first letter of the alphabet, it reaches the very beginning of all beings. *Aleph*—the name for the first letter of the Hebrew alphabet—consists of the same letters as *pele* which is the term for both wonder and mystery. . . .

A person who prays too loudly has not arrived at the highest realm, the realm of the mystery. He has only a sense for the obvious and apparent, and whatever is apparent is not attached to the highest realm, for what is highest is hidden."[20]

Praise is our first response. Aflame with inability to say what His presence means, we can only sing, we can only utter words of adoration.

This is why in Jewish liturgy *praise* rather than *petition* ranks foremost. It is the more profound form, for it involves not so much the sense of one's own dependence and privation as the

[20]Rabbi Loew of Prague, *Netivoth Olam, netiv haavodah,* Ch. 2.

sense of God's majesty and glory.[21] In praising Him all that is specious, all that is false, is dispelled. We rise to a higher level of living.

> *For to Thee*
> *Lord our God*
> *God of our fathers,*
> *are due*
> *songs and praise,*
> *hymn and psalm,*
> *power and dominion,*
> *victory,*
> *grandeur, might,*
> *homage, beauty,*
> *holiness, kingship,*
> *blessings, thanksgiving.*
>
> (The daily liturgy)

Our worship is humble; our superlatives are understatements.

The Polarity of Prayer

There is a specific difficulty of Jewish prayer. There are laws: how to pray, when to pray, what to pray. There are fixed times, fixed ways, fixed texts.[22] On the other hand, prayer is worship of the heart, the outpouring of the soul, a matter of *kavanah* (inner devotion). Thus, Jewish prayer is guided by two opposite principles: order and outburst, regularity and spontaneity, uni-

[21]Significantly, prayers written in our time are essentially petitional. Prayers of praise often sound like self-praise.

[22]According to Rabbi Yose, "He who alters the form of benedictions fixed by the wise has failed to fulfil his obligations" (*Berachoth* 40b; *Yerushalmi Berachoth* VI, 2, 10b). Rabbi Meir declares it to be the duty of everyone to say one hundred benedictions daily (*Menahoth* 43a, see *Numbers Rabba*, XVIII).

formity and individuality, law and freedom,[23] a duty and a pre-rogative,[24] empathy and self-expression, insight and sensitivity, creed and faith, the word and that which is beyond words.[25] These principles are the two poles about which Jewish prayer revolves. Since each of the two moves in the opposite direction, equilibrium can only be maintained if both are of equal force. However, the pole of regularity usually proves to be stronger than the pole of spontaneity, and, as a result, there is a perpetual danger of prayer becoming a mere habit, a mechanical perform-ance, an exercise in repetitiousness. The fixed pattern and regu-larity of our services tends to stifle the spontaneity of devotion. Our great problem, therefore, is how not to let the principle of regularity impair the power of spontaneity (*kavanah*). It is a problem that concerns not only prayer but the whole sphere of Jewish observance. He who is not aware of this central difficulty is a simpleton; he who offers a simple solution is a quack.

It is a problem of universal significance. Polarity is an essen-tial trait of all things in reality, and in Jewish faith the relation-ship between *halacha* (law) and *agada* (inwardness) is one of *polarity*. Taken abstractly they seem to be mutually exclusive, yet in actual living they involve each other. Jewish tradition main-tains that there is no *halacha* without *agada* and no *agada* with-out *halacha;* that we must neither disparage the body nor sacri-fice the spirit. The body is the discipline, the pattern, the law; the spirit is the inner devotion, spontaneity, freedom. The body without the spirit is a corpse; the spirit without the body is a ghost.

And yet the polarity exists and is a source of constant anxiety

[23]The contrast between order and spontaneity is made clear through the term *keva*. Shammai said: "Make your *Torah* (in the sense of legal decisions made by the scholar) *keva* (a fixed thing)." Do not be lenient to yourself and severe to others, nor lenient to others and severe to yourself. See *Aboth* 1, 15 and the explication in *Aboth de Rabbi Nathan*, ed. Schechter, B ver-sion, Ch. 23, p. 47. In contrast Rabbi Shimeon said: "When you pray, do not make your prayer a fixed thing" (*keva*) (Aboth 2, 18). Rabbi Eliezer said: "He who makes his prayer a fixed thing (*keva*), his prayer is not an act of grace (*Mishnah Berachoth* 4, 4)."

[24]See p. 67.
[25]See above, p. 37.

and occasional tension. How are we to maintain the reciprocity of tradition and freedom; how to retain both *keva* and *kavanah*, regularity and spontaneity, without upsetting the one or stifling the other?

At first sight, the relationship between *halacha* and *agada* in prayer appears to be simple. Tradition gives us the text, we create the *kavanah*. The text is given once and for all, the inner devotion comes into being every time anew. The text is the property of all ages, *kavanah* is the creation of a single moment. The text belongs to all men, *kavanah* is the private concern of every individual. And yet, the problem is far from being simple. The text comes out of a book, it is given; *kavanah* must come out of the heart. But is the heart always ready—three times a day—to bring forth devotion? And if it is, is its devotion in tune with what the text proclaims?

The Primacy of Inwardness

In regard to most aspects of observance, Jewish tradition has for pedagogic reasons given primacy to the principle of *keva*; there are many rituals concerning which the law maintains that if a person has performed them without proper *kavanah*, he is to be regarded *ex post facto* as having fulfilled his duty. In prayer, however, *halacha* insists upon the primacy of inwardness, of *kavanah* over the external performance, at least, theoretically.[26] Thus, Maimonides declares: "Prayer without *kavanah* is no prayer at all. He who has prayed without *kavanah* ought to pray once more. He whose thoughts are wandering or occupied with other things need not pray until he has recovered his mental composure. Hence, on returning from a journey, or if one is weary or distressed, it is forbidden to pray until his mind is composed. The sages said that upon returning from a journey, one should

[26]The polarity of prayer and a decision in favor of the element of *kavanah* is implied in the discussion whether prayer is "supplication" or "a substitute for sacrifice," *Berachoth*, 26a.

66

wait three days until he is rested and his mind is calm, then he prays."[27]

Prayer is not a service of the lips; it is worship of the heart. "Words are the body, thought is the soul, of prayer." If one's mind is occupied with alien thoughts, while the tongue moves on, then such prayer is like a body without a soul, like a shell without a kernel. Such a person may be compared to a servant whose master returned home. The servant urged his wife and the members of his family to show honor to the master and provide for all his needs, while he himself went out to loiter in the market-place.[28]

Significantly, Nahmanides, in contrast to other authorities, insists that *prayer is not a duty*, but a prerogative, and he who prays does not perform a requirement of the law. It is not the law of God that commands us to pray; it is the love and "grace of the Creator, blessed be He, to hear and to answer whenever we call upon Him."[29]

In reality, however, the element of regularity has often gained the upper hand over the element of spontaneity. Prayer has become lip service, an obligation to be discharged, something to get over with. "This people draw near, with their mouth and with their lips do honor Me, but have removed their heart far from Me and their fear of Me is a commandment of Me learned by rote."[30]

The primacy of inwardness in prayer may be explained by a parable. There was once a king who commanded his servants to make him savory food such as he loved. So they brought him the dish and he ate. And even though the preparation of the dish required many different kinds of work such as cutting wood, drawing water, slaughtering animals, kindling fire, cleaning pots and pans, and cooking, nevertheless the king only commanded them concern the savory food. And if it would have been possible to have produced the morsel without these steps, his

[27]*Mishneh Torah*, Tefillah, 4, 6.
[28]Bahya Ibn Paquda, *The Duties of the Heart*, ed. by Harmson, Vol. IV, p. 71.
[29]Nahmanides, *Notes on Maimonides' Sefer Hamitzoth*, mitzvah 5.
[30]Isaiah 29:13.

commandment would still have been considered fulfilled. For the king was not interested in the wood or the water and he was not concerned with the way the food is made.

Now imagine what would happen if, when the time to eat arrived, the servants were to come in carrying pots and pans. And when the king asked, "What are these?" they were to say to him: "You have told us to make savory food for you. Here, sir, is the equipment with which they are made." Indeed would not the king burn with anger and would he not rightly say to them: "I commanded you only to bring me savory food. Did I ask you for pots and pans?"[31]

And so it is with words of prayer when the heart is absent. Prayer becomes trivial when ceasing to be an act in the soul. The essence of prayer is *agada, inwardness.* Yet it would be a tragic failure not to appreciate what the spirit of *halacha* does for it, raising it from the level of an individual act to that of an eternal intercourse between the people Israel and God; from the level of an occasional experience to that of a permanent covenant. It is through *halacha* that we belong to God not occasionally, intermittently, but essentially, continually. Regularity of prayer is an expression of my belonging to an order, to the covenant between God and Israel, which remains valid regardless of whether I am conscious of it or not.

How grateful I am to God that there is a duty to worship, a law to remind my distraught mind that it is time to think of God, time to disregard my ego for at least a moment! It is such happiness to belong to an order of the divine will. I am not always in a mood to pray. I do not always have the vision and the strength to say a word in the presence of God. But when I am weak, it is the law that gives me strength; when my vision is dim, it is duty that gives me insight.[32]

We must not think, that *kavanah* is a small matter. It requires constant effort, and we may fail more often than we succeed. But the battle for *kavanah* must go on, if we are not to die of spiritual paralysis.

[31]Rabbi Menahem Lonzano, *Derech Hayim,* Lemberg, 1931, p. 84.
[32]See p. 97.

To offer an example: In order to prevent the practice of repeating a prayer for superstitious or magical purposes, the Talmud ordains that a person who says the word "*Hear*" (*O Israel*) or the word "*We thank Thee*" twice, is to be silenced. Rab Pappa asked Abbai: But perhaps the person repeated his prayer because when he said the words the first time he did not have *kavanah*. So he repeated the prayer in order to say it with *kavanah*. Thus, there was no ground for suspecting him of indulging in superstition or magical practices. Why should we silence him? Answered Abbai: "Has anyone intimacy with heaven?" Has anyone the right to address God thoughtlessly as one talks to a familiar friend? "If he did not at first direct his mind to prayer, we smite him with a smith's hammer until he does direct his mind."[33]

Prayer is not for the sake of something else. *We pray in order to pray.* It is the queen of all commandments. No religious act is performed in which prayer is not present. No other *mitzvah* (commandment; a sacred act) enters our lives as frequently, as steadily, as the majesty of prayer.

The first tractate of the Talmud, the first section of Maimonides' Code as well as Caro's code, deal with prayer. We are told that "prayer is greater than good deeds," "more precious than . . . sacrifices."[34] To Rabbenu Bahya ben Asher, the spiritual sphere that prayer can reach is higher than the sphere out of which inspiration of the prophets flows.[35]

The philosophy of Jewish living is essentially a philosophy of worship. For what is observance, if not a form of worshiping God?

What is a *mitzvah*, a sacred act? *A Prayer in the form of a deed.*

This is the way of finding out whether we serve God, or an idea of God—through prayer. It is the test of all we are doing. What is the difference between Torah and *Wissenschaft des Judentums*? If an idea we have clarified, a concept we have

[33]*Berachoth* 33b–34a.

[34]*Berachoth* 32a.

[35]Rabbi Bahya ben Asher, *Commentary on the Pentateuch*, on Deuteronomy 11:12.

evolved, turns into a prayer, it is Torah. If it proves to be an aid to praying with greater *kavanah,* it is Torah; otherwise it is *Wissenschaft.* Prayer is of no importance unless it is of supreme importance. It is one of the things which *"stand on the summit of the world,"* transcending the world and ascending to God, "and which men treat lightly."[36]

"The hour of worship is both the core and the mature fruit of one's time, while all other hours are like the channels leading to it . . . they stand in the same relation to the soul as food to the body. Prayer is to the soul what nourishment is to the body, and the blessing one derives from prayer lasts until it is time to pray again, just as the strength derived from the midday meal lasts till the evening meal."[37]

Prayer Is Sacrifice

Prayer is more than meditation, and reading the prayers involves more than reproducing vocally, while following their symbols with the eyes, the words of the liturgy. A third-century scholar avers that it is improper to call upon the person who acts as the reader of prayers for the congregation by saying, *Come and pray;* we must rather use the words, *Come, karev.* Since the Hebrew word *karev* has four meanings, the invitation extended to him signifies the four tasks which a reader has to fulfill. *Karev* means

   —offer our sacrifices!
   —satisfy our needs!
   —wage our battles!
   —bring us close to Him![38]

The statement that since the destruction of the Temple in Jerusalem, prayer has taken the place of sacrifice, does not imply that sacrifice was abolished when the sacrificial cult went out

---

[36]*Berachoth* 6a.

[37]Rabbi Jehuda Halevi, *Kuzari,* V, 5.

[38]*Jerushalmi Berachoth* IV, 4, 8b; and Jacob Levy, *Neuhebraeisches und Chaldaeisches Woerterbuch,* Vol. IV, p. 368b.

of existence. Prayer is not a substitute for sacrifice. Prayer *is* sacrifice. What has changed is the substance of sacrifice: the self took the place of the thing. The spirit is the same.

"Accept the offerings of praise, O Lord," says the Psalmist (119:108). "Let my prayer be counted as incense before Thee, and the lifting of my hands as an evening sacrifice" (141:2). In moments of prayer we try to surrender our vanities, to burn our insolence, to abandon bias, cant, envy. We lay all our forces before him. The word is but an altar. We do not sacrifice. We are the sacrifice.

During the act of prayer, one must "place himself among those who are ready to sacrifice themselves for the sanctification of God's Name, by reciting with proper devotion the confession of unity, *Hear, O Israel*. Then he must make himself poor, when he knocks at the door of the highest heights by saying the prayer, *True and certain*, and proceed thus to the *Amidah* (the silent prayer), so that he, in saying it, should feel himself brokenhearted, poor, needy. Then he should place himself among the saints by recounting his sins in the prayer *Hearkening to prayer*. So he should do in order to cling to the right hand ["of God"] which is stretched forth to receive sinners who repent."[39]

To the saints, prayer is a hazard, a venture full of peril. Every person who prays is a priest at the greatest of all temples. The whole universe is the temple. With good prayer he may purify it, with improper prayer he may contaminate it. With good prayer he may "build worlds," with improper prayer he may "destroy worlds." According to Rabbi Ami, a man's prayer is answered only if he stakes his very life on it.[40] "It is a miracle that a man survives the hour of worship," the Baal Shem said. Before every morning prayer Rabbi Uri of Strelisk would take leave of his household, telling them what should be done with his manuscripts if he should pass away while praying.

The readiness to make the supreme sacrifice for the sake of His holy name, for the sake of the truth that *God is One*, has long

[39]*Zohar*, Vol. II, p. 195b (English translation, London, The Soncino Press, 1934).

[40]*Taanith* 8a.

been the essence of our devotion in proclaiming, *Hear, O Israel*. When following the Bar Kochba rebellion, the Roman government prohibited the teaching of Torah, the great Rabbi Akiba continued to expound the words of God and to convey them to others. Thereupon he was arrested and eventually condemned to the hand of the executioner.

"When the Romans brought Rabbi Akiba out to execution, it was time for reading the *Shema;* and though they were combing his flesh with iron combs, he continued to take upon himself the yoke of the Kingship of heaven," he continued to read the words of the Shema: *Hear, O Israel, the Lord is our God, the Lord is One. Thou shalt love the Lord thy God with all thy heart, with all thy soul, with all thy might.* His disciples said to him:

—Our master, thus far! (Although suffering such agonies, you still say the *Shema!*) And Rabbi Akiba answered them:

—Throughout my life I have been troubled with this verse, *'And thou shalt love the Lord, thy God . . . with all thy soul,'* which means: Even if he take thy life. For said I, 'When will it be in my power to fulfill it?' Now that the opportunity is mine, shall I not fulfill it?

He prolonged the word *ehad* ["One" in "Hear, O Israel"], until his soul left [the body] with the word *ehad* [on his lips]. A heavenly Voice issued forth and announced, 'Happy art thou, Rabbi Akiba, that thy soul went out with the word *ehad.*'"[41]

As we said above, prayer has the power to generate insight, it endows us often with understanding not attainable by speculation. Prayer is a way to faith. Some of mankind's deepest spiritual insights are born in moments of prayer. The following letter may serve as an illustration.[42]

[41]*Berachoth* 61b.

[42]The author of the letter, written in Hebrew, Rabbi Eisik Epstein of Homel in Russia (1780?–1856?) was a disciple of the "old master," the founder of the *Habad* school within the hasidic movement, Rabbi Shneur Zalman of Ladi (1745–1813) and of his son, Rabbi Baer (died 1827). The letter was written before the year 1827.

A Letter About Faith

I remember the days of old, when the love that we had for each other was like the love one has for his own soul. How could I refrain from speaking to you? . . .

Listen to me, my beloved brother. Do not think that what I say is heresy or philosophy. What I am going to say is the essence of faith which has the power to revive the dead and through which even dry bones can feel the living God.

All *hasidim*, particularly the disciples of our great Master, whose soul is in heaven, have attained the kind of faith [which I will now describe]. It is something we discover and experience particularly in the "Silent prayer," following all the meditations in the "Psalms of Praise," and in the Shema. Then comes the faith and the insight that *All is God*.[43] And the darkness of "the world of confusion," of the confusion of good and evil, retreats from our sight. One still realizes that the world is as it was, [that nothing external has changed], but it does not matter, it does not affect one's faith. . . .

Such insight, such faith may be attained in one of two ways.

[43]The phrase "all is God" is not reversable; it must not be confused with pantheism. It must be understood in the context of the *Habad* teachings. According to Rabbi Shneur Zalman of Ladi (see *Shaar Hayichud Vehaemunah,* Chapters 2 and 3), the work of God who created heaven and earth is not to be thought of as being analogous to the work of man. Once a craftsman has made a vessel, it no longer depends on him for its existence. "Fools imagine that heaven and earth are likewise made . . . but they fail to see the vast difference between the work of man, which consists of making one thing out of another already existing, and the work of the Creator who creates being out of nothing." The miracle of coming into being out of nothing is only possible through the continual action of God. His power is constantly present within all His creations, and were He to remove Himself for a moment they would revert to their natural state, which is nothingness. However, because that Divine power or light is concealed, it appears to us as if they exist by themselves.

In a true sense, therefore, the world that we know is nothing compared with the Power of God that contains it. Things appear to us to be existing by themselves, only as long as we are unable to perceive the Divine.

Either by being exceedingly contrite, exceedingly lowly, because of the realization of how insensitive we are to the truth that is so manifest and in full sight. Or by warming oneself in the light of such faith, even if it is [still] beyond us. . . .

Such faith is given to all *hasidim*. In their opponents, the *mitnagdim* . . . faith exists in utter obscurity, shrouded and vague. They have the kind of faith which the children of Israel had when they were slaves in Egypt. For them, God is all things to all people. They will believe anything and everything about Him, but they have no capacity for the belief that all is God.

Hasidim always have such faith. The hasidim of old, the disciples of Rabbi Nahum of Tshernobil,[44] would be carried away to violent ecstasies by such faith. This was due to the fact they had neglected the way of analysis and reflection. In the disciples of our Master such faith exists in greater lucidity and refinement. They achieve that inhight while praying as described above [namely, from meditation to experience]. These flashes of insight that there is nothing but He alone, that all is God, come and go, penetrate and retreat, come forth and withdraw, but they know that this is the way all emanation proceeds—the light flows out of Him and the light streams back perpetually, from the uppermost heights to the nethermost depths.

However, such faith is still on a *lower* level. It is of the same kind as a child's knowledge of his father. Both the child and the adult know well who their father is. The knowledge of the adult has no greater claim to truth than the knowledge of the child. There is only one difference. The child does not know how or why or by what process this person is his father; his knowledge is no knowledge in the strict sense, nor does he have any need of exact knowledge. In contrast, the adult knows clearly and distinctly how and why and by what process that person came to beget him. However, the exact knowledge of the adult, a knowledge from reason, is contingent upon simple child-like knowledge. If he lacks child-like knowledge that this person is his father, he will fail to realize that it is this person from whose substance and essence he is derived. Consequently, the knowledge of the adult is not an achievement of reason alone.

[44] A disciple of the Baal Shem and of the Great Maggid, he died in 1798.

74

What is true of man and his father is true of man and God. The roots of his *higher* faith in God are not in the realm of reason but in the divine soul[45] [with which man is endowed] which, when perfected, becomes aware of its faith with clarity and distinction. What the divine soul achieves is not a speculative insight but pure faith. . . .

This *higher* kind of faith is engraved on our souls like subtle exquisite figures engraved on translucent glass. He who looks casually sees nothing. He who looks carefully sees that something is engraved on it. Yet, unless he applies ointments to improve his vision, he will not perceive clearly what he sees. . . .

It follows, then, that two things are necessary. One, to look persistently, and two, to consult a competent doctor whose medicine can correct one's faulty vision. Such treatment one received in absorbing the good and precious words of hasidic guidance which our [old] Master and teacher, whose soul is in heaven, would utter. His words were a healing to the divine soul in us and called forth its power to understand its own [higher] faith with clarity and distinction. This power came to us not because his words had the sweetness of lucidity. It was the light that radiated from his holy words that enabled the soul to understand with clarity and distinction that all is God. Even when the world, perceived at the very moment of his speaking to us, was enveloped in darkness, we sensed: All is God.

To find such faith I strained every fiber in me and expended every ounce of my strength.

Our Master and teacher, his soul is in heaven, placed in me the seed of faith when delivering his discourse, *ten women shall bake your bread in one oven* (Leviticus 26:26).[46] It was still the lower kind of faith. But that faith began to sprout and to bloom under the guidance of his son (and his successor), our Master and teacher. However, my eyes were too weak and my own strength insufficient to nurture it. I was craving intensely for more direct and personal guidance. And so I sent numerous appeals and petitions [requesting a personal interview], but our Master

[45]See Rabbi Shneur Zalman of Ladi, *Tanya, Likkute Amarim*, Ch. 9.

[46]The discourse is found in Rabbi Shneur Zalman, *Likkute Torah*, ad locum.

and teacher refused to see me privately. I went through much anguish and distress, until my entreaty was finally answered. . . . How could I convey what he said? . . . I stood there spellbound, oblivious to time and space. After he had finished, it was as if a beam of light had pierced my very being like an arrow. . . . I was ready to go out in the streets and to shout: All is God, yet for some reason I decided that I must not do it. I do not recall the reason anymore. . . . Believe me, as God lives and as my soul lives, I do not exaggerate a bit. . . .

Spiritual Delicacy

My intention is not to offer blueprints, to prescribe new rules— except one: Prayer must have life. It must not be a drudgery, something done in a rut, something to get over with. It must not be fiction, it must not be flattened to a ceremony, to an act of mere respect for tradition.

If the main purpose of being a rabbi is to bring men closer to their Father in heaven, then one of his supreme tasks is to pray and to teach others how to pray. Torah, worship and charity are the three pillars upon which the world rests. To be a man implies the acceptance of *the pre-eminence of prayer*.

To be able to inspire people to pray one must love his people, understand their predicaments and be sensitive to the power of exaltation, purification and sanctification hidden in our prayer book. To attain such sensitivity he must commune with the great masters of the past, and learn how to pour his own dreams and anxieties into the well of prayer.

We must learn to acquire the basic virtues of inwardness which alone qualify a person to be a *mentor of prayer*.

One of these virtues is a sense of *spiritual delicacy*. *Vulgarity* is deadness to delicacy; the sin of incongruity; the state of being insensitive to the hierarchy of living, to the separation of private and public, of intimate and social, of sacred and profane, of farce and reverence.

In itself no act is vulgar; it is the incongruity of the circumstances, the mixing up of the spheres, the right thing in the wrong context, the out-of-placeness, that generates vulgarity. The use of devices proper in merchandizing for influencing opinion about the truth of a scientific theory; bringing to public notice a matter that belongs to the sphere of intimate life is vulgar.[47]

For us, it is of vital importance to beware of *intellectual vulgarity*. Many categories, conceptions or words that are properly employed in the realm of our political, economic, or even scientific activities are, when applied to issues such as God or prayer, an affront to the spirit. Let us never put the shoes in the Ark; let us try to regain a sense of separation (*havdalah*), of spiritual delicacy. Let us recapture the meaning of separation (*le-havdil*). There is no sense of sanctity without a sense of separation. Every week we initiate the Sabbath by *an act of sanctification* (*kiddush*) and conclude the Sabbath by *an act of separation* (*havdalah*, from the rest of the week).

An Ontological Necessity

The problem is not how to revitalize prayer; the problem is how to revitalize ourselves. Let us begin to cultivate those thoughts and virtues without which our worship becomes, of necessity, a prayer for the dead—for ideas which are dead to our hearts.

We must not surrender to the power of platitudes. If our

[47]A good illustration is the rabbinic dictum: "All know for what purpose a bride is brought into the bridal chamber, but whoever disgraces his mouth and utters an unchastity—even if a divine decree of seventy years of happiness were sealed [and granted] unto him, it is turned for him into evil," *Ketuboth* 8b. In 1954 the following advertisement appeared in a New York magazine. "How to pray and get results. . . . Learn *The Magic Formula for Successful Prayer*. . . . 10-Day Trial. Just send your name and address. . . . $1 plus postage. . . . I positively *guarantee* that you will be more than delighted with *results* within 10 days or your money will be returned promptly."

rational methods are deficient and too weak to plumb the depth of faith, let us go into stillness and wait for the age in which reason will learn to appreciate the spirit rather than accept standardized notions that stifle the mind and stultify the soul. We must not take too seriously phrases or ideas which the history of human thought must have meant in jest, as for example, that prayer is "a symbol of ideas and values," "a tendency to idealize the world," "an act of the appreciation of the self." There was a time when God became so distant that we were almost ready to deny Him, had psychologists or sociologists not been willing to permit us to believe in Him. And how grateful some of us were when told *ex cathedra* that prayer is not totally irrelevant because it does satisfy an emotional need.

To Judaism the purpose of prayer is not to satisfy an emotional need. Prayer is not a need but *an ontological necessity,* an act that constitutes the very essence of man.[48] He who has never prayed is not fully human. Ontology, not psychology or sociology, explains prayer.

The dignity of man consists not in his ability to make tools, machines, guns, but primarily in his being endowed with the gift of addressing God. It is this gift which should be a part of the definition of man.[49]

We must learn how to study the inner life of the words that fill the world of our prayer book. Without intense study of their meaning, we feel, indeed, bewildered when we encounter the multitude of those strange, lofty beings that populate the inner cosmos of the Jewish spirit. It is not enough to know how to translate Hebrew into English; it is not enough to have met a word in the dictionary and to have experienced unpleasant adventures with it in the study of grammar. A word has a soul, and we must learn how to attain insight into its life.

This is our affliction—we do not know how to look across a word to its meaning. We forgot how to find the way to the word, how to be on intimate terms with a few passages in the prayer book. Familiar with all words, we are intimate with none.

[48]Rabbi Jehuda Loew ben Bezalel (Maharal) of Prague (died 1609), *Netivoth Olam,* Haavodah.
[49]Compare *Midrash Tehillim 4, 5.*

As a result, we say words but make no decisions, forgetting that in prayer words are commitments, not the subject matter for esthetic reflection, that prayer is meaningless unless we stand for what we utter, unless we feel what we accept. *A word of prayer is a word of honor given to God.* However, we have lost our sense for the earnestness of speech, for the dignity of utterance. Spiritual life demands the sanctification of speech. Without an attitude of piety toward words, we will remain at a loss how to pray.

Moreover, words must not be said for the sake of stiffening the mind, of tightening the heart. They must open the mind and untie the heart. A word may be either a blessing or a misfortune. As a blessing it is the insight of a people in the form of a sound, a store of meaning accumulated throughout the ages. As a misfortune it is a substitute for insight, a pretext or a cliché. To those who remember, many of the words in our liturgy are still warm with the glow of our fathers' devotion. Such people we must inspire to recall. While those who have no such memory we must teach how to sense the spiritual life that pulsates through the throbbing words.

Preach in Order to Pray

In the light of such a decision about the pre-eminence of prayer, the role as well as the nature of the sermon will have to be re-examined. The prominence given to the sermon as if the sermon were the core and prayer the shell, is not only a drain on the intellectual resources of the preacher but also a serious deviation from the spirit of our tradition. The sermon, unlike prayer, has never been considered as one of the supreme things in this world. If the vast amount of time and energy invested in the search of ideas and devices for preaching; if the fire spent on the altar of oratory were dedicated to the realm of prayer, we would not find it too difficult to convey to others what it means to utter a word in the presence of God.

Preaching is either an organic part of the act of prayer or out of place. Sermons indistinguishable in spirit from editorials in the *New York Times*, urging us to have faith in the *New Deal, the Big Three* or *the United Nations,* or attempting to instruct us in the latest theories of psychoanalysis, will hardly inspire us to go on to the *musaf* (the last part of the service) and to vow,

> *Through all generations*
> *we will declare Thy greatness;*
> *To all eternity*
> *we will proclaim Thy holiness;*
> *Thy praise, our God,*
> *shall never depart from our mouth.*

Preach in order to pray. Preach in order to inspire others to pray. The test of a true sermon is that it can be converted to prayer.

To the average worshiper many texts of perennial significance have become vapid and seem to be an assembly line of syllables. It is, therefore, a praiseworthy custom for the rabbi to bring forth the meaning of the prayers to the congregation. Unfortunately, some rabbis seem to think that their task is to teach popular science, and as a result some services are conducted as if they were *adult-education* programs. Dwelling on the historical aspects, they discuss, for example, the date of composition of the prayers, the peculiarities of their literary form or the supposedly primitive origin of some of our laws and customs.

What about the spirit of prayer? What about relating the people to the truth of its ideas? Too often, so-called explanation kills inspiration.[50] The suggestion that the Day of Atonement grew out of a pagan festival is, regardless of its scientific merit,

---

[50] I am informed that a congregation listening to comments delivered before the *havdalah* was told the following: "At the conclusion of the Sabbath, when the additional soul departs, one must be refreshed by smelling aromatic herbs, for at that moment, according to the *Zohar*, 'the soul and spirit are separated and sad until the smell comes and unites them and makes them glad.' However, this is, of course, not the true reason. The authentic origin of the ceremony is that in ancient times people ate a great deal on the Sabbath and a bad odor came out of their mouth. In order to drive out the odor, they used spices."

hardly consonant with the spirit of *"Kol Nidre"* (the evening service of the Day of Atonement).

Nor must prayer be treated as an ancestral institution. In explaining sections of the prayer book, our task is not to give a discourse about quaint customs or about "the way our fathers used to think." The liturgy is not a museum of intellectual antiquities and the synagogue is not a house of lectureship but a house of worship. The purpose of such comments is to inspire "outpouring of the heart" rather than to satisfy historical curiosity; to set forth the hidden relevance of ideas rather than hypotheses about forgotten origins.

The Unknown Book

There is a book which everyone talks about, but few people have really read—a book which has the distinction of being one of the least known books in our literature. It is *the prayer book.* Countless moments of insight can be gained by communing with its individual words. The same word may evoke new understanding when read with an open heart. There is light in the words, but we ignore it. Almost any word, any passage, has untold resources of meaning, paradoxical beauty and depth. How many of us have ever pondered over the very first word of Psalms 145? What superhuman boldness to say *"I will extol Thee, my God O King,"* and yet we say it three times each day. What a paradox for me to promise to lift up Him who is the Most High. . . .

Let us consider another example:

> *Sing unto the Lord a new song;*
> *Sing unto the Lord, all the earth.*
> Psalms 96:1
>
> *Praise Him, sun and moon,*
> *Praise Him, all you shining stars.*
> Psalms 148:3

The Egyptian priest could not call upon the stars to praise the gods. He believed that the soul of Isis sparkled in Sirius, the

81

soul of Horus in Orion, and the soul of Typhon in the Great Bear; it was beyond his scope to conceive that all beings stand in awe and worship God. In our liturgy we go beyond a mere hope; every seventh day we proclaim as a fact: *The soul of everything that lives blesses Thy name.*[51]

> *They all thank Thee,*
> *They all praise Thee,*
> *They all say,*
> *There is none holy like the Lord.*

Whose ear has ever heard how all trees sing to God? Has our reason ever thought of calling upon the sun to praise the Lord? And yet, what the ear fails to perceive, what reason fails to conceive, our prayer makes clear to our souls. It is a higher truth, to be grasped by the spirit:

> *All Thy works praise Thee*
> Psalms 145:10

We are not alone in our acts of praise. Wherever there is life, there is silent worship. The world is always on the verge of becoming one in adoration. It is man who is the cantor of the universe, and in whose life the secret of cosmic prayer is disclosed.

The trouble with the prayer book is: it is too great for us, it is too lofty. Since we have failed to introduce our minds to its greatness, our souls are often lost in its sublime wilderness.

The liturgy has become a foreign language even to those of us who know Hebrew. It is not enough to know the vocabulary; what is necessary is to understand the categories, the way of thinking of the liturgy. It is not enough to read the words; what is necessary is to answer them.

What is our liturgy as a whole trying to express if not the basic realities and attitudes of Jewish faith? To worship is to experience, not only to accept these realities and attitudes. The liturgy is our creed in the form of *a spiritual pilgrimage.* We do not confess our belief in God; we adore Him. We do not proclaim

[51]The usual translation "shall bless" totally misses the meaning of the passage.

82

our belief in revelation; we utter our gratitude for it. We do not formulate the election of Israel; we sing it. Thus our liturgy is no mere memorial to the past; it is an act of participating in Israel's bearing witness to the unity, uniqueness, love and judgment of God. It is an act of joy.

It is reported of a certain rabbi that after each prayer he would recite with great joy the words of the Psalmist (66:20): *Blessed be God who has not taken away from me the ability to pray nor withheld His grace from me.*[52]

Our prayer book is going to remain obscure unless Jewish teachers will realize that one of their foremost tasks is to discover, to explain and to interpret the words of the prayer book. What we need is *a sympathetic prayer book exegesis.*

Religious movements in our history have often revolved around the problem of liturgy. In the modern movements, too, liturgy has been a central issue.

But there was a difference. To Kabbalah and Hasidism the primary problem was *how to pray;* to the modern movements, the primary problem was *what to say.* What has Hasidism accomplished? It has inspired worship in a vast number of Jews. What have the moderns accomplished? They have inspired the publication of a vast number of prayer books. It is important for the rabbis to clarify their goal. Is it to make a contribution to bibliography or to endow our people with a sense of *kavanah*? There have been numerous *Prayer Book* Commissions. Why is there no *Prayer* Commission?

Modern Jews suffer from a neurosis which I should like to call *the Siddur (prayer book) complex.*

True, the text of the prayer book presents difficulties to many people. But the crisis of prayer is not a problem of the text. It is a problem of the soul. The *Siddur* must not be used as a scapegoat. A revision of the prayer book will not solve the crisis of prayer. What we need is a revision of the soul, a new heart rather than a new text. Textual emendations will not save the

[52]Rabbi Menahem Brody, *Baer Menachem* preface, Nyiregyhaza, 1937. See Ibn Ezra ad locum.

spirit of prayer. Nothing less than a spiritual revolution will save prayer from oblivion.

The Nature of *Kavanah*

Kavanah is more than attentiveness, more than the state of being aware of what we are saying. If *kavanah* were only presence of the mind, it would be easily achieved by a mere turn of the mind. Yet, according to the Mishnah, the pious men of old felt that they had to meditate an hour in order to attain the state of *kavanah*. In the words of the Mishnah, *kavanah* means "to direct the heart to the text or the content of the prayer."[53] *Kavanah*, then, is more than paying attention to the literal meaning of a text. It is *attentiveness to God, an act of appreciation of being able to stand in the presence of God.*

Appreciation is not the same as reflection. It is one's being drawn to the preciousness of something he is faced with. To sense the preciousness of being able to pray, to be perceptive of the supreme significance of worshiping God is the beginning of higher *kavanah*.

"Prayer without *kavanah* is like a body without a soul." "A word uttered without the fear and love of God does not rise to heaven." Once Rabbi Levi Yitzhak of Berdythev, while visiting a city, went to a synagogue. Arriving at the gate he refused to enter. When his disciples inquired what was wrong with the synagogue, they received the reply: "The synagogue is full of words of Torah and prayer." This seemed the highest praise to his disciples, and even more reason to enter the synagogue. When they questioned him further, Rabbi Levi Yitzhak explained: "Words uttered without fear, uttered without love, do not rise to heaven. I sense that the synagogue is full of Torah and full of prayer."

[53]Rabbenu Yonah, *Commentary on Alfassi, Berachoth,* Ch. 4, beginning.

84

Judaism is not *a religion of space*.[54] To put it more sharply, it is *better* to have *prayer without a synagogue than a synagogue without prayer*.[55] And yet we always speak of *synagogue attendance* rather than of prayer. It is the right word for the wrong spirit. By being in the space of a synagogue while a service is being conducted one has not fulfilled his religious duty. Many of those attending Sabbath services arrive during the reading of the weekly Torah portion and leave without having read the *Shema* or prayed the "silent prayer" (of *shaharith*)—the two most important parts of the prayer.

Nor is it the primary purpose of prayer "to promote Jewish unity." As we said above, prayer is a personal duty, and an intimate act which cannot be delegated to either the cantor or the whole community. We pray with the whole community, and every one of us by himself. We must make clear to every Jew that his duty is to pray rather than to be a part of an audience.

Thirty Centuries of Experience

The rabbi's role in the sacred hour of worship goes far beyond that of maintaining order and decorum. His unique task is to be a source of inspiration, to endow others with a sense of *kavanah*. And as we have said, *kavanah* is more than a touch of emotion. *Kavanah* is insight, appreciation. To acquire such insight, to deepen such appreciation, is something *we must learn* all the days of our lives. It is something *we must live* all the days of our lives. Such insight, such appreciation, we must convey to

[54]Rabbi Hama ben Hanina and Rabbi Oshaya were strolling near the synagogue of Lud. Rabbi Hama boasted: "How much money have my ancestors invested in these buildings!" Rabbi Oshaya replied: "How many souls have they wasted here! Were there no students of Torah to support instead?"

Rabbi Abin donated a gate to the Great Synagogue. When Rabbi Mana came to him, he boasted: "Do you see what I have done?" Said Rabbi Mana: "'When Israel forgets its Creator, they build temples' (Hosea 8:14). Were there no students of Torah to support instead?" *Shekalim*, Ch. 5, end.

[55]*Midrash Tehillim*, 4, 9; see above, p. 38.

others. It may be difficult to convey to others *what we think,* but it is not difficult to convey to others *what we live.* Our task is to echo and to reflect the light and spirit of prayer.

What I plead for is the creation of a prayer atmosphere. Such an atmosphere is not created by ceremonies, gimmicks or speeches, but by the example of prayer, by a person who prays. You create that atmosphere not around you but within you. I am a congregant and I know from personal experience how different the situation is when the rabbi is concerned with prayer instead of with how many people attend the service; the difference between a service in which the rabbi comes prepared to respond to thirty centuries of Jewish experience and one in which he comes to review the book of the month or the news of the day.

It was in the interest of bringing about order and decorum that in some synagogues the rabbi and cantor decided to occupy a position facing the congregation. It is quite possible that a re-examination of the whole problem of worship would lead to the conclusion that the innovation was an error. The essence of prayer is not decorum but rather an event in the inner life of men. "He who prays must turn his eyes down and his heart up."[56] What goes on in the heart is reflected in one's face. It is embarrassing to be exposed to the sight of the whole congregation in moments when one wishes to be alone with his God.

A cantor who faces the holiness in the Ark rather than the curiosity of man will realize that his audience is God. He will learn to realize that his task is not to entertain but to represent the people Israel. He will be carried away into moments in which he will forget the world, ignore the congregation and be overcome by the awareness of Him in Whose presence he stands. The congregation then will hear and sense that the cantor is not giving a recital but worshiping God, that to pray does not mean to listen to a singer but to identify oneself with what is being proclaimed in their name.[57]

Kavanah requires preparation. Miracles may happen, but one must not rely on miracles. The spirit of prayer is frequently

[56]*Yebamoth* 105b. See Rabbi Judah's view and Rashi's comment, *Rosh Hashanah,* 26b.

[57]Rabbi Israel Ibn Al-Nakawa, *Menorat Hamaor,* ed. by H. G. Enelow, New York, 1929, Vol. 2, p. 84.

decided during the hour which precedes the time of prayer. Negatively, one is not ready to engage in certain activities, or even in light talk before he prays. And positively one must learn to perform a degree of inner purification before venturing to address the King of kings. According to Maimonides, "One must free his heart from all other thoughts and regard himself as standing in the presence of the *Shechinah*. Therefore, before engaging in prayer, the worshiper ought to go aside a little in order to bring himself into a devotional frame of mind, and then he must pray quietly and with feeling, not like one who carries a weight and throws it away and goes farther."[58]

Let us pray the way we talk. Let us not just utter consonants and vowels. Let us learn how to chant our prayers. It is one of our tragedies that we did not know how to appreciate the very soul of our ancient speech, the chant, and instead, have adopted a pompous monotonous manner. Let us try to recapture the last traces of our ancient chant. Let us learn to *express* what we say.

The Issue of Prayer Is Not Prayer

To repeat, the issue of prayer is not prayer; the issue of prayer is God. It has often been claimed in modern times that Judaism has no theology, that it does not matter what a person means by the word God, as long as he believes that there is a God. Now, is it really of no importance what we mean by God? What is God? An empty generality? An alibi? Some kind of an idea that we develop? I have been wrestling with the problem all my life as to whether I really mean God when I pray to Him, whether I have even succeeded in knowing what I am talking about and whom I am talking to. I still don't know whether I serve God or I serve something else. Unfortunately, many of us pick up any term developed by any philosopher, long after that philosophy itself has already died in the history of philosophy, and give it the name of God.

The question may be asked what our attitude should be toward the prayer of those who do not accept the ancient conception

[58]*Mishneh Torah*, Tefillah, 4, 16.

of God that is discussed. Now the issue is not the formulation *of a concept* or the acceptance of a definition. We Jews have no concepts; all we have is faith, faith in His willingness to listen to us. We have no information, but we sense and believe in His being near to us. Israel is not a people of definers of religion but *a people of witnesses* to His concern for man.

We have committed ourselves to Jewish experience, let us not distort it. We are not ready to emend the text and begin the "silent prayer" by saying, "Blessed be It, the Supreme Concept, the God of Spinoza, Dewey and Alexander." Indeed, the term "God of Abraham, Isaac and Jacob" is semantically different from a term such as "the God of truth, goodness and beauty." Abraham, Isaac and Jacob do not signify ideas, principles or abstract values. Nor do they stand for teachers or thinkers, and the term is not to be understood like that of "the God of Spinoza, Dewey and Alexander." The categories of the Bible are not principles to be comprehended but events to be continued. The life of him who joins the covenant of Abraham continues the life of Abraham. Abraham endures for ever. We *are* Abraham, Isaac, Jacob.

There are no concepts which we could appoint to designate the greatness of God or represent Him to our minds. He is not a being whose existence can be proved by our syllogisms. He is a reality, in the face of which, when becoming alive to it, all concepts become clichés.

Genuine prayer does not flow out of concepts. It comes out of the awareness of the mystery of God rather than out of information about Him.

There is no one who has no theology. It is the false theologies silencing God that block and hamper us in our response to Him. It is our misdirected certainty and unfounded dogma that have stifled the heart of Jewish prayer. Everyone today will grant that there is a supreme deity that has ultimate power in the realm of being and values. But why is not God also granted the power to penetrate human lives? The power to reach the people of Israel? Is He only omnipotent in general but not in fact? It is just as wrong to place Him beyond all the beyonds as it once was to see Him inside every stone. He who claims to know that

God is trapped in a closed system of silent unrelatedness, that He is behind the bars of infinity, that He cannot address us, is more dogmatic than I. With this kind of dogmatism we have to take issue.

As said above, unless God is at least as real as my own self, unless I am sure that God has at least as much life as I do, how could I pray? If God does not have the power to speak to us, how should we possess the power to speak to Him? If God is unable to listen to me, then I am insane in talking to Him.

The strange thing about many of our contemporaries is that their life is nobler than their ideology, that their faith is deep and their views are shallow, that their souls are suppressed and their slogans proclaimed. We must not continue to cherish a theory, just because we have embraced it forty years ago. Faith is not something that we acquire once and for all. Faith is an insight that must be acquired at every single moment.

Be Afraid, and Pray

Those who honestly search, those who yearn and fail, we did not presume to judge. Let them pray to be able to pray, and if they do not succeed, if they have no tears to shed, let them yearn for tears, let them try to discover their heart and let them take strength from the certainty that this too is a high form of prayer.

A learned man lost all his sources of income and was looking for a way to earn a living. The members of his community, who admired him for his learning and piety, suggested to him to serve as their cantor on the Days of Awe. But he considered himself unworthy of serving as the messenger of the community, as the one who should bring the prayers of his fellow-men to the Almighty. He went to his master the Rabbi of Husiatin and told him of his sad plight, of the invitation to serve as a cantor on the Days of Awe, and of his being afraid to accept it and to pray for his congregation.

"Be afraid, and pray," was the answer of the rabbi.[59]

59 A. J. Heschel, *Man Is Not Alone*, p. 256.

4

Continuity Is
the Way

The Goal and The Way

Unfree men are horrified by the suggestion of accepting a daily discipline. Confusing inner control with external tyranny, they prefer caprice to self-restraint. They would rather have ideals than norms, hopes than directions, faith than forms. But the goal and the way cannot long endure in separation. The days of the week, the food that we eat, the holidays of the year, the deeds that we do—these are the frontiers of faith. Unless the outer life expresses the inner world, piety stagnates and intention decays.

Man is constantly producing words and deeds, giving them

over either to God or to the forces of evil. Every move, every detail, every act, every effort to match the spiritual and the material, is serious. The world is not a derelict; life is not a neutral ground. In this life of ours the undirected goes astray, the haphazard becomes chaotic, what is left to chance is abandoned.

We have said that prayer is the quintessence of the spiritual life, that is, the climax of aspirations. But faith cannot be satisfied with climaxes. It cannot rest content with essences. Faith knows no boundaries between the will of God and all of life. Therefore, we have been taught to care for the meaning that is found in deeds, to sense the holy that is available in the everyday, to be devoted to the daily as much as to the extraordinary, to be concerned for the cycle as much as for the special event.

Before we prayed, we may have thought prayer to be a hobby that could be pursued on occasion. After prayer, we know that prayer is a privilege, to be earned through existence. To pray what we sense, we must live what we pray. Since man is both body and soul, both "his heart and his flesh should sing to the Living God." Since the inner world is sacred, the outer world must be kept clean. Since the goal is great, the way must be directed.

Our problem is how to live what we pray, how to make our lives a daily commentary on our prayer book, how to live in consonance with what we promise, how to keep faith with the vision we pronounce. We turn therefore to a study of the law, to an analysis of the meaning of observance.

From the Point of View of God

I came with great hunger to the University of Berlin to study philosophy. I looked for a system of thought, for the depth of the spirit, for the meaning of existence. Erudite and profound scholars gave courses in logic, epistemology, esthetics, ethics and metaphysics. They opened the gates of the history of philosophy. I was exposed to the austere discipline of unremitting inquiry and self-criticism. I communed with the thinkers of the past who

94

knew how to meet intellectual adversity with fortitude, and learned to dedicate myself to the examination of basic premises at the risk of failure.

Yet, in spite of the intellectual power and honesty which I was privileged to witness, I became increasingly aware of the gulf that separated my views from those held at the university. I had come with a sense of anxiety: how can I rationally find a way where ultimate meaning lies, a way of living where one would never miss a reference to supreme significance? Why am I here at all, and what is my purpose? I did not even know how to phrase my concern. But to my teachers that was a question unworthy of philosophical analysis.

I realized my teachers were prisoners of a Greek-German way of thinking. They were fettered in categories which presupposed certain metaphysical assumptions which could never be proved. The questions I was moved by could not even be adequately phrased in categories of their thinking.

My assumption was: man's dignity consists in his having been created in the likeness of God. My question was: how must man, a being who is in essence the image of God, think, feel and act? To them, religion was a feeling. To me, religion included the insights of the Torah which is a vision of man from the point of view of God. They spoke of God from the point of view of man. To them God was an idea, a postulate of reason. They granted Him the status of being a logical possibility. But to assume that He had existence would have been a crime against epistemology.

The problem to my professors was how to be good. In my ears the question rang: how to be holy. At the time I realized: There is much that philosophy could learn from Jewish life. To the philosophers: the idea of the good was the most exalted idea, the ultimate idea. To Judaism the idea of the good is pen-ultimate. It cannot exist without the holy. The good is the base, the holy is the summit. Man cannot be good unless he strives to be holy.

To have an idea of the good is not the same as living by the insight, *Blessed is the man who does not forget Thee.*

I did not come to the university because I did not know the idea of the good, but to learn why the idea of the good is valid, why and whether values had meaning. Yet I discovered that values sweet to taste proved sour in analysis; the prototypes were firm, the models flabby. Must speculation and existence remain like two infinite parallel lines that never meet? Or perhaps this impossibility of juncture is the result of the fact that our speculation suffers from what is called in astronomy a parallax, from the apparent displacement of the object, caused by the actual change of our point of observation?

God's Desire That I Worship

In those months in Berlin I went through moments of profound bitterness. I felt very much alone with my own problems and anxieties. I walked alone in the evenings through the magnificent streets of Berlin. I admired the solidity of its architecture, the overwhelming drive and power of a dynamic civilization. There were concerts, theatres, and lectures by famous scholars about the latest theories and inventions, and I was pondering whether to go to the new Max Reinhardt play or to a lecture about the theory of relativity.

Suddenly I noticed the sun had gone down, evening had arrived.

From what time may one recite the Shema in the evening?[1]

I had forgotten God—I had forgotten Sinai—I had forgotten that sunset is my business—that <u>my task is "to restore the world to the kingship of the Lord."</u>

So I began to utter the words of the evening prayer.

Blessed art thou, Lord our God,
King of the universe,
who by His word brings on the evenings. . . .

And Goethe's famous poem rang in my ear:

[1]The first words of the *Mishna* dealing with the evening prayer. On *Shema* see above, p. 36, note 9.

96

Ueber allen Gipfeln ist Ruh'
O'er all the hilltops is quiet now.

No, that was pagan thinking. To the pagan eye the mystery of life is *Ruh'*, death, oblivion.[2]

To us Jews, there is meaning beyond the mystery. We would say

O'er all the hilltops is the word of God.

The meaning of life is to do His will. . . . And I uttered the words,

Who by His word brings on the evenings.

And His love is manifested in His teaching us Torah, precepts, laws:

Ueber allen Gipfeln is God's love for man—.

Thou hast loved the house of Israel with everlasting love.
Thou hast taught us Torah, mitzvot, laws, rules. . . .

How much guidance, how many ultimate insights are found in our liturgy.

How grateful I am to God that there is a duty to worship, a law to remind my distraught mind that it is time to think of God, time to disregard my ego for at least a moment! It is such happiness to belong to an order of the divine will.

I am not always in a mood to pray. I do not always have the vision and the strength to say a word in the presence of God. But when I am weak, it is the law that gives me strength; when my vision is dim, it is duty that gives me insight.

Indeed, there is something which is far greater than my desire to pray, namely, God's desire that I pray. There is something which is far greater than my will to believe, namely, God's will that I believe. How insignificant is my praying in the midst of a cosmic process! Unless it is the will of God that I pray, how ludicrous is it to pray.

On that evening in the streets of Berlin, I was not in a mood

[2]Goethe characterized himself as an "old pagan." Once he exclaimed, "We want to remain pagans. Long live paganism!" Goethe's Gespräche, II (1909), pp. 354, 356; see, however, p. 62.

to pray. My heart was heavy, my soul was sad. It was difficult for the lofty words of prayer to break through the dark clouds of my inner life.

But how would I dare not to *pray?* How would I dare to miss an evening prayer? "Out of *emah*, out of fear of God do we read the *Shema*." (*me-emah-thai*, the first word of the tractate *Berachoth*, Rabbi Levi Yizhak.)

I Will Betroth You to Myself Forever

The following morning I awoke in my student room. Now, the magnificent achievements in the field of physiology and psychology have, of course, not diminished, but rather increased my sense of wonder for the human body and soul. And so I prayed

Blessed be Thou . . . who hast formed man in
wisdom . . .
My God, the soul which Thou hast placed within
me is pure . . .

Yet how am I going to keep my soul clean?

The most important problem which a human being must face daily is: How to maintain one's integrity in a world where power, success and money are valued above all else? How to remain clean amidst the mud of falsehood and malice that soil our society?

The soul is clean, but within it resides a power for evil, "a strange god,"[3] that "seeks constantly to get the upper hand over man and to kill him; and if God did not help him, he could not resist it, as it is said, 'the wicked watches the righteous, and seeks to slay him.' "[4]

Every morning I take a piece of cloth—neither elegant nor solemn, of no particular esthetic beauty, a prayer-shawl, wrap myself in it and say:

[3]*Shabbath* 105b.
[4]*Sukkah* 52b.

98

"How precious is Thy kindness, O God! The children of man take refuge in the shadow of Thy wings. They have their fill of the choice food of Thy house, and Thou givest them drink of Thy stream of delights. For with Thee is the fountain of life; by Thy light do we see light. Continue Thy kindness to those who know Thee, and Thy righteousness to the upright in heart."

But, then, I ask myself: Have I got a right to take my refuge in Him? to drink of the stream of His delights? to expect Him to continue His kindness? But God wants me to be close to Him, even to bind every morning His word as a sign on my hand, and between my eyes. I would remind myself of the word that God spoke to *me* through His prophet Hosea:

"I will betroth you unto Me forever; I will betroth you unto Me in righteousness and in justice, in kindness and in mercy. I will betroth you unto Me in faithfulness; and you shall know the Lord" (Hosea 2:21–22). It is an act of betrothal, a promise to marry. . . . It is an act of God, falling in love with His people. But the engagement depends on righteousness, justice, kindness, mercy.

The Loss of the Whole

Why did I decide to take religious observance seriously in spite of the numerous perplexities in which I became enmeshed?

Why did I pray, although I was not in a mood to pray? And why was I able to pray in spite of being unprepared to pray? What was my situation after the reminder to pray the evening prayer struck my mind? The duty to worship stood as a thought of ineffable meaning; doubt, the voice of disbelief, was ready to challenge it. But where should the engagement take place? In an act of reflection the duty to worship is a mere thought, timid, frail, a mere shadow of reality, while the voice of disbelief is a power, well-armed with the weight of inertia and the preference for abstention. In such an engagement prayer would be fought *in absentia,* and the issue would be decided without actually joining the battle. It was fair, therefore, to give the weaker rival a chance: to pray first, to fight later.

I realized that just as you cannot study philosophy through praying, you cannot study prayer through philosophizing. And what applies to prayer is true in regard to the essentials of Jewish observance.

What I wanted to avoid was not only the failure to pray to God during a whole evening of my life but *the loss of the whole,* the loss of belonging to the spiritual order of Jewish living. It is true that some people are so busy with collecting shreds and patches of the law, that they hardly think of weaving the pattern of the whole. But there is also the danger of being so enchanted by the whole as to lose sight of the detail. It became increasingly clear to me that the order of Jewish living is meant to be, not a set of rituals, but an order of all of man's existence, shaping all his traits, interests and dispositions; "not so much the performance of single acts, the taking of a step now and then, as the pursuit of a way, being on the way; not so much the acts of fulfilling as the state of being committed to the task, the belonging to an order in which single deeds, aggregates of religious feeling, sporadic sentiments, moral episodes become a part of a complete pattern" (270).[5]

The ineffable Name, we have forgotten how to pronounce it. We have almost forgotten how to spell it. We may totally forget how to recognize it.

To Obey or To Play with the Will of God

There are a number of ideas concerning Jewish law which have proved most inimical to its survival. Let us discuss two of these. First is the assumption that either you observe all or nothing; all of its rules are of equal importance; and if

[5]Numbers in parentheses in this chapter refer to pages of the author's *Man Is Not Alone.*

one brick is removed, the whole edifice must collapse. Such intransigence, laudable as it may be as an expression of devoutness, is neither historically nor theologically justified. There were ages in Jewish history when some aspects of Jewish ritual observance were not adhered to by people who had otherwise lived according to the law. And where is the man who could claim that he has been able to fulfill literally the *mitzvah* of "Love thy neighbor as thyself"?

Where is the worry about the spiritual inadequacy of that which admittedly should not be abandoned? Where is our anxiety about the barrenness of our praying, the conventionality of our obedience?

The problem, then, that cries for a solution is not everything or nothing, total disregard or obedience to the law; the problem is authentic or forged, genuine or artificial observance. The problem is not *how much* but *how to* observe. The problem is whether we *obey* or whether we merely *play* with the word of God.

Second is the assumption that every iota of the law was revealed to Moses at Sinai. This is an unwarranted extension of the rabbinic concept of revelation. "Could Moses have learned the whole Torah? Of the Torah it says, *Its measure is longer than the earth, and broader than the sea* (Job 11:9); could, then, Moses have learned it in forty days? No, it was only the principles thereof (*kelalim*) which God taught Moses."[6]

The role of the sages in interpreting the word of the Bible and their power to issue new ordinances are basic elements of Jewish belief and something for which our sages found sanction in Deuteronomy 17:11. The awareness of the expanding nature of Jewish law was expressed by such a great saint and authority as Rabbi Isaiah Horovitz in his *Two Tablets of the Covenant.*

"And now I will explain the phenomenon that in every generation the number of restrictions [in the law] is increased. In the time of Moses, only what he had explicitly received at Sinai (the written law) was binding, plus several ordinances which he added for whatever reasons he saw fit. [However] the prophets, the Tannaim, and the rabbis of every generation [have continued

[6]*Exodus Rabba*, 41, 6. See Rabbi Yom Tov Lipmann Heller, *Tosefoth Yom Tov*, preface.

to multiply these restrictions]. The reason is, that as the filth of the serpent spreads, greater protection is needed. The Holy One provided for us three hundred and sixty-five prohibitions in order to prevent the filth from becoming too active. Therefore, whenever the filth of a generation grows squalid, more restrictions must be imposed. Had this [the spread of filth] been the situation at the time of the giving of the Torah, [those interdictions] would have been specifically included in it. However, instead the later ordinances derive their authority from God's command—'make a protection for the law'—which means 'make necessary ordinances according to the state of each generation' and these have the same authority as the Torah itself."[7]

There are times in Jewish history when the main issue is not what parts of the law cannot be fulfilled but what parts of the law can be and ought to be fulfilled, fulfilled as law, as an expression and interpretation of the will of God.

There are many problems which we encounter in our reflections on the issue of Jewish observance. I would like to discuss briefly several of these problems, namely, the relation of observance to our understanding of the will of God; the meaning of observance to man; the regularity of worship; inwardness and the essence of religion; the relevance of the external deeds.

Does God Require Anything of Man?

From a rationalist's point of view it does not seem plausible to assume that the infinite, ultimate supreme Being is concerned with my putting on Tefillin every day. It is, indeed, strange to believe that God should care whether a particular individual will eat leavened or unleavened bread during a particular season of the year. However, it is that paradox, namely, that the infinite God is intimately concerned with finite man and his finite deeds; that nothing is trite or irrelevant in the eyes of God, which is the very essence of the prophetic faith.

[7] *Shne Luhoth Haberith*, 25b.

There are people who are hesitant to take seriously the possibility of our knowing what the will of God demands of us. Yet we all wholeheartedly accept Micah's words: "He has showed you, O man, what is good, and what does the Lord require of you, but to do justice, and to love kindness and to walk humbly with your God" (Micah 6:8). If we believe that there is something which God requires of man, then what is our belief if not *faith in the will of God, certainty of knowing what His will demands of us?* If we are ready to believe that God requires of me "to do justice," is it more difficult for us to believe that God requires of us to be holy? If we are ready to believe that it is God who requires us "to love kindness," is it more difficult to believe that God requires us to hallow the Sabbath and not to violate its sanctity?

If it is the word of Micah uttering the will of God that we believe in, and not a peg on which to hang views we derived from rationalist philosophies, then "to love justice" is just as much law as the prohibition of making a fire on the Seventh Day. If, however, all we can hear in these words are echoes of Western philosophy rather than the voice of Micah, does that not mean that the prophet has nothing to say to any of us?

A Leap of Action

A serious difficulty is the problem of *the meaning of Jewish observance.* The modern Jew cannot accept the way of static obedience as a short-cut to the mystery of the divine will. His religious situation is not conducive to an attitude of intellectual or spiritual surrender. He is not ready to sacrifice his liberty on the altar of loyalty to the spirit of his ancestors. He will only respond to a demonstration that there is meaning to be found in what we expect him to do. His primary difficulty is not in his inability to comprehend the *Divine origin* of the law; his essential

103

difficulty is in his inability to sense *the presence of Divine meaning* in the fulfillment of the law.

Let us never forget that some of the basic theological presuppositions of Judaism cannot be justified in terms of human reason. Its conception of the nature of man as having been created in the likeness of God, its conception of God and history, of prayer and even of morality, defy some of the realizations at which we have honestly arrived at the end of our analysis and scrutiny. The demands of piety are a mystery before which man is reduced to reverence and silence. In a technological society, when religion becomes a function, piety, too, is an instrument to satisfy his needs. We must, therefore, be particularly careful not to fall into the habit of looking at religion as if it were a machine which can be worked, an organization which can be run according to one's calculations.

The problem of how to live as a Jew cannot be solved in terms of common sense and common experience. The order of Jewish living is a spiritual one; it has a spiritual logic of its own which cannot be apprehended unless its basic terms are lived and appreciated.

It is in regard to this problem that we must keep in mind three things. (a) Divine meaning is *spiritual* meaning; (b) the apprehension of Divine meaning is contingent upon *spiritual preparedness;* (c) it is experienced in *acts,* rather than in speculation.

(a) The problem of ethics is: what is the ideal or principle of conduct that is *rationally* justifiable? While to religion the problem of living is: what is the ideal or principle of living that is *spiritually* justifiable? The legitimate question concerning the forms of Jewish observance is, therefore, the question: Are they spiritually meaningful?

We should, consequently, not evaluate the *mitzvoth* (commandments and religious acts) by the amount of rational meaning we may discover at their basis. Religion is not within but beyond the limits of mere reason. Its task is not to compete with reason, to be a source of speculative ideas, but to aid us where reason gives us only partial aid. Its meaning must be understood in terms *compatible with the sense of the ineffable.* Frequently where concepts fail, where rational understanding ends, the meaning of observance begins. Its purpose is not essentially to serve hygiene, happiness or the vitality of man; its purpose is to add holiness to hygiene, grandeur to happiness, spirit to vitality.

Spiritual meaning is not always limpid; transparency is the quality of glass, while diamonds are distinguished by refractive power and the play of prismatic colors.

Indeed, any reason we may advance for our loyalty to the Jewish order of living merely points to one of its many facets. To say that the *mitzvoth* have meaning is less accurate than saying that they lead us to wells of emergent meaning, to experiences which are full of hidden brilliance of the holy, suddenly blazing in our thoughts.

Those who, out of their commendable desire to save the Jewish way of life, bring its meaning under the hammer, tend to sell it at the end to the lowest bidder. The highest values are not in demand and are not saleable on the market-place. In spiritual life some experiences are like a *camera obscura,* through which light has to enter in order to form an image upon the mind, the image of ineffable intelligibility. Insistence upon explaining and relating the holy to the relative and functional is like lighting a candle in the camera.

Works of piety are like works of art. They are functional, they serve a purpose, but their essence is intrinsic, their value is in what they are in themselves.

(b) Sensitivity to spiritual meaning is not easily won; it is the fruit of hard, constant devotion, of insistence upon remaining true to a vision. It is "an endless pilgrimage . . . a drive towards serving Him who rings our hearts like a bell, as if He were waiting to enter our lives. . . . Its essence is not revealed in the way we utter it, but in the soul's being in accord with what is relevant to God; in the extension of our love to what God may approve, our being carried away by the tide of His thoughts, rising beyond the desolate ken of man's despair" (174).

"God's grace resounds in our lives like a staccato. Only by retaining the seemingly disconnected notes comes the ability to grasp the theme" (88).

(c) What is the Jewish way to God? It is not a way of ascending the ladder of speculation. Our understanding of God is not the triumphant outcome of an assault upon the riddles of the universe nor a donation we receive in return for intellectual surrender. Our understanding comes by the way of *mitzvah* (religious act). By living as Jews we attain our faith as Jews. We do not have faith in deeds; we attain faith through deeds.

When Moses recounted to the people the laws of the covenant with God, the people responded: "We will do and we will hear." This statement was interpreted to mean: *In doing we perceive.*

A Jew is asked to take *a leap of action* rather than *a leap of thought:* to surpass his needs, to do more than he understands in order to understand more than he does. In carrying out the word of the Torah he is ushered into the presence of spiritual meaning. Through the ecstasy of deeds he learns to be certain of the presence of God.

Jewish law is a sacred prosody. The Divine sings in our deeds, the Divine is disclosed in our deeds. Our effort is but a counterpoint in the music of His will. In exposing our lives to God we discover the Divine within ourselves and its accord with the Divine beyond ourselves.

If at the moment of doing a *mitzvah* once perceived to be thus sublime, thus Divine, you are in it with all your heart and with all your soul, there is no great distance between you and God. For acts of holiness uttered by the soul disclose the holiness of God hidden in every moment of time. And his holiness and He are one.

Routine Breeds Attention

Why should worship be bound to regular occasions? Why impose a calendar on the soul? Is not regularity of observance a menace to the freedom of the heart?

Strict observance of a way of life at fixed times and in identical forms tends to become a matter of routine, of outward compliance. How to prevent observance from becoming stereotyped, mechanical, was, indeed, a perennial worry in the history of

Judaism. The cry of the prophet: "Their heart is far from me" was a signal of alarm.

Should I reject the regularity of prayer and rely on the inspiration of the heart and only worship when I am touched by the spirit? Should I resolve: unless the spirit comes, I shall abstain from praying? The deeper truth is that routine breeds attention, calling forth a response where the soul would otherwise remain dormant. One is committed to being affected by the holy, if he abides at the threshold of its realm. Should it be left to every individual to find his own forms of worship whenever the spirit would move him? Yet who is able to extemporize a prayer without falling into the trap of clichés? Moreover, spiritual substance grows in clinging to a source of spirit richer than one's own.

Inspirations are brief, sporadic and rare. In the long interims the mind is often dull, bare and vapid. There is hardly a soul that can radiate more light than it receives. To perform a *mitzvah* is to meet the spirit. But the spirit is not something we can acquire once and for all but something we must constantly live with and pray for. For this reason the Jewish way of life is to reiterate the ritual, to meet the spirit again and again, the spirit in oneself and the spirit that hovers over all beings.

The spirit rests not only on our achievement, on our goal, but also on our effort, on our way. This is why the very act of going to the house of worship, every day or every seventh day, is a song without words. When done in humility, in simplicity of heart, it is like a child who, eager to hear a song, spreads out the score before its mother. All the child can do is to open the book.[8]

But the song must be forthcoming. We cannot long continue to live on a diet that consists of anticipation plus frustration.

By Faith Alone?

At the root of our difficulties in appreciating the role of the law in religious living is, I believe, our conception of the very essence of religion. "We are often inclined to define the essence

[8]See above, p. 68

of religion as a state of the soul, as inwardness, as an absolute feeling, and expect a person who is religious to be endowed with a kind of sentiment too deep to rise to the surface of common deeds, as if religion were a plant that can only thrive at the bottom of the ocean. Now to Judaism religion is not a feeling for something that is, but *an answer* to Him who is asking us to live in a certain way. *It is in its very origin a consciousness of duty, of being committed to higher ends;* a realization that life is not only man's but also God's sphere of interest" (175).

"God asks for the heart." Yet does he ask for the heart only? Is the right intention enough? Some doctrines insist that love is the sole condition for salvation (the Sufis, Bhakti-mārga), stressing the importance of inwardness, of love or faith, to the exclusion of good works.

Paul waged a passionate battle against the power of law and proclaimed instead the religion of grace. Law, he claimed, cannot conquer sin, nor can righteousness be attained through works of law. A man is justified "by faith without the deeds of the law."[9]

That salvation is attained by faith alone was Luther's central thesis. The antinomian tendency resulted in the overemphasis on love and faith to the exclusion of good works.

The Formula of Concord of 1580 condemns the statement that good works are necessary to salvation and rejects the doctrine that they are harmful to salvation. According to Ritschl, the doctrine of the merit of good deeds is an intruder in the domain of Christian theology; the only way of salvation is justification by faith. Barth, following Kierkegaard, voices Lutheran thoughts, when he claims that man's deeds are too sinful to be good. There are fundamentally no human deeds, which, because of their significance in this world, find favor in God's eyes. God can be approached through God alone.

[9]Romans 3:28. "By the deeds of the law there shall no flesh be justified in his sight; for by the law is knowledge of sin." An argument against the Lutheran doctrine of "the justification by faith alone" is made by Walter Lowrie, *What Is Christianity?*, New York, 1953, pp. 77–90.

Absolute Relevance of Human Deeds

Paraphrasing the Paulinian doctrine that man is saved by faith alone, Kant and his disciples taught that the essence of religion or morality would consist in an absolute quality of the soul or the will, regardless of the actions that may come out of it or the ends that may be attained. Accordingly, the value of a religious act would be determined wholly by the intensity of one's faith or by the rectitude of one's inner disposition. The intention, not the deed, the *how*, not the *what* of one's conduct, would be essential, and no motive other than the sense of duty would be of any moral value. Thus, acts of kindness, when not dictated by the sense of duty, would not be better than cruelty; while compassion or regard for human happiness as such is looked upon as an ulterior motive. "I would not break my word even to save mankind," exclaimed Fichte. As if his own salvation and righteousness were more important to him than the fate of all men. Does not such an attitude illustrate the truth of the proverb: "The road to hell is paved with good intentions"? Should we not say that a concern with one's own salvation and righteousness that outweighs the regard for the welfare of one other human being, cannot be qualified as a good intention?

The crisis of ethics has its root in formalism, in the view that the essence of the good is in the good intention. Seeing how difficult it is to attain it, modern man despaired. In the name of good intentions, evil was fostered.

To us this doctrine is the essential heresy. Judaism stands and falls with the idea of the absolute relevance of human deeds. Even to God we ascribe the deed. *Imitatio dei* is in deeds. The deed is the source of holiness.

"Faith does not come to an end with attaining certainty of God's existence. Faith is the beginning of intense craving to enter an active relationship with Him who is beyond the mystery, to bring together all the might that is within us with all that is spiritual beyond us. At the root of our yearning for integrity is a stir of the inexpressible within us to commune with the ineffable beyond us. But what is the language of that communion, without which our impulse remains inarticulate?

"We are taught that what God asks of man is more than an inner attitude, that He gives man not only *life* but also *a law*, that His will is to be served not only adored, *obeyed* not only *worshiped*. Faith comes over us like a force urging to action. We respond by pledging ourselves to constancy of devotion, committing us to the presence of God. This remains a life allegiance involving restraint, submission, self-control and courage.

"Judaism insists upon establishing a unity of *faith* and *creed*, of *piety* and *halacha* (law), of *devotion* and *deed*. Faith is but a seed, while the deed is its growth or decay. Faith disembodied, faith that tries to grow in splendid isolation, is but a ghost, for which there is no place in our psychophysical world.

"What *creed* is in relation to *faith*, the *halacha* is in relation to *piety*. As faith cannot exist without a creed, piety cannot subsist without a pattern of deeds; as intelligence cannot be separated from training, religion cannot be divorced from conduct. Judaism is lived in deeds, not only in thoughts.

"A pattern for living—the object of our most urgent quest— which would correspond to man's ultimate dignity, must take into consideration not only his ability to exploit the forces of nature and to appreciate the loveliness of its forms, but also his unique sense of the ineffable. It must be a design, not only for the satisfaction of needs, but also for the attainment of an end," the end of being *a holy people* (175–76).

There Is No Exterritoriality

The integrity of life is not exclusively a thing of the heart, and Jewish piety is, therefore, more than consciousness of the moral law. The innermost chamber must be guarded at the uttermost outposts. Religion is not the same as spiritualism; what man does

110

in his concrete physical existence is directly relevant to the divine. Spirituality is the goal, not the way of man. In this world music is played on physical instruments, and to the Jew the *mitzvoth* are the instruments by which the holy is performed. If man were only mind, worship in thought would be the form in which to commune with God. But man is body and soul, and his goal is to live so that both "his heart and his flesh should sing to the living God."

Moreover, worship is not one thing, and living, another. Does Judaism consist of sporadic landmarks in the realm of living, of temples in splendid isolation, of festive celebrations on extraordinary days? The synagogue is not a retreat, and that which is decisive is not the performance of rituals at distinguished occasions, but how they affect the climate of the entire life.

The highest peak of spiritual living is not necessarily reached in rare moments of ecstasy; the highest peak lies wherever we are and may be ascended in a common deed. There can be as sublime a holiness in fulfilling friendship, in observing dietary laws, day by day, as in uttering a prayer on the Day of Atonement.

Jewish tradition maintains that there is no exterritoriality in the realm of the spirit. Economics, politics, dietetics are just as much as ethics within its sphere. It is in man's intimate rather than public life, in the way he fulfills his physiological functions that character is formed. It is immensely significant that, according to the Book of Genesis, the first prohibition given to man concerned the enjoyment of the forbidden fruit.

"The fate of a people . . . is decided according to whether they begin culture at the right place—not at the soul. The right place is the body, demeanor, diet, physiology; the rest follows . . . contempt of the body is the greatest mishap." Judaism begins at the bottom, taking very seriously the forms of one's behavior in relation to the external, even conventional, functions and amenities of life, teaching us how to eat, how to rest, how to act. The discipline of feelings and thoughts comes second. The body must be persuaded first. "Thou shalt not covet" is the last of the Ten Commandments, even though it may be the first in the case history of the aforementioned transgressions. While

111

not prescribing a diet—vegetarian or otherwise—or demanding abstinence from narcotics or stimulants, Judaism is very much concerned with what and how a person ought to eat. A sacred discipline for the body is as important as bodily strength.

Lest We Burn the Bridge

In order to attain an adequate appreciation of the preciousness that the Jewish way of living is capable of bestowing upon us, we should initiate a thorough cleaning of the minds. Every one of us should be asked to make one major sacrifice: to sacrifice his prejudice against our heritage. We should strive to cultivate an atmosphere in which the values of Jewish faith and piety could be cherished, an atmosphere in which the Jewish form of living is the heartily approved or at least respected pattern, in which sensitivity to *kashruth* (dietary laws) is not regarded as treason against the American Constitution and reverence for the Sabbath is not considered conspiracy against progress.

Without solidarity with our forebears, the solidarity with our brothers will remain feeble. The vertical unity of Israel is essential to the horizontal unity of *kelal* Israel (the community of Israel). Identification with what is undying in Israel, the appreciation of what was supremely significant throughout the ages, the endeavor to integrate the abiding teachings and aspirations of the past into our own thinking will enable us to be creative, to expand, not to imitate or to repeat. Survival of Israel means that we carry on our independent dialogue with the past. Our way of life must remain such as would be, to some degree, intelligible to Isaiah and Rabbi Yochanan ben Zakkai, to Maimonides and the Baal Shem.

Let us be under no illusion. The task is hard. However, if it is true that the good cannot exist without the holy, what are we doing for the purpose of securing holiness in the world? Can we afford to be indifferent, to forget the responsibility which our position as teachers bestows upon us?

A wide stream of human callousness separates us from the realm of holiness. Neither an individual man nor a single gen-

112

eration can by its own power erect a bridge that would reach that realm. For ages our fathers have labored in building a sacred bridge. *We who have not crossed the stream must beware lest we burn the bridge.*

"Customs and Ceremonies"

Prompted by an intuition that we cannot live by a disembodied faith, many people today speak of the advisability of introducing "rituals, customs, and ceremonies." Many groups advocate a return to *symbolism and ceremonialism* because of the poetry and beauty, the mysticism and the drama which they provide.

Is this approach in the spirit of prophetic Judaism? Is it symbolism that God desires? Is it ceremonialism that the prophets called for? Are *"customs and ceremonies"* the central issue of Jewish observance? *"Customs and ceremonies"* are an external affair, an esthetic delight; something cherished in academic fraternities or at graduation exercises at universities.

But since when has esthetics become the supreme authority in matters of religion? Customs, ceremonies are fine, enchanting, playful. But is Judaism a religion of play? What is the authentic origin of these terms—*customs and ceremonies?* I must confess that I have difficulty translating "ceremonies" into Hebrew. Customs—*minhagim*—have given us a lot of trouble in the past. *Minhagim* have often stultified Jewish life. According to Rabbenu Tam, the consonants of the Hebrew word for custom, *minhag*, when read backwards, mean hell, *gehinom.*[10]

Let us beware lest we reduce Bible to literature, Jewish observance to good manners, the Talmud to Emily Post.

There are spiritual reasons which compel me to feel alarmed when hearing the terms *customs and ceremonies.* What is the worth of celebrating the Seder on Passover Eve if it is nothing but a ceremony? An annual re-enactment of quaint antiquities?

[10]Compare the references in the *Year Book of the Central Conference of American Rabbis,* Vol. LXIII (1953), p. 406.

Ceremonies end in boredom, and boredom is the great enemy of the spirit.

A religious act is something in which the soul must be able to participate; out of which inner devotion, *kavanah,* must evolve. But what *kavanah* should I entertain if entering the *sukkah* is a mere ceremony?

Let us be frank. Too often a ceremony is the homage which disbelief pays to faith. Do we want such homage?

Judaism does not stand on ceremonies . . . Jewish piety is an answer to God, expressed in the language of *mitzvoth* rather than in the language of *ceremonies and symbols.* The *mitzvah* rather than the ceremony is our fundamental category. What is the difference between the two categories?

Ceremonies whether in the form of things or in the form of actions are required by custom and convention; *mitzvoth* are required by Torah. Ceremonies are relevant to man; *mitzvoth* are relevant to God. Ceremonies are folkways; *mitzvoth* are ways to God. Ceremonies are expressions of the human mind; what they express and their power to express depend on a mental act of man; their significance is gone when man ceases to be responsive to them. Ceremonies are like the moon, they have no light of their own. *Mitzvoth,* on the other hand, are *expressions or intrepretations* of the will of God. While they are meaningful to man, the source of their meaning is not in the understanding of man but in the love of God. Ceremonies are created for the purpose of *signifying: mitzvoth* were given for the purpose of *sanctifying.* This is their function: to refine, to ennoble, to sanctify man. They confer holiness upon us, whether or not we know exactly what they signify.

A *mitzvah* is more than *man's reference to God;* it is also *God's reference to man.* In carrying out a *mitzvah* we acknowledge the fact of God being concerned with our fulfillment of His will.

Ceremonialism is a part of a great issue, the issue of symbolism which has come to dominate religious thinking of our day. Modern man no longer knows how to encounter reality face to face. To him the world of reality is known only through graphs and charts, tools and signs. It is, therefore, the problem of symbolism to which we must turn.

114

5

Symbolism

I. SPATIAL SYMBOLS

Art and Religion

From time immemorial man has been concerned with the question how to create a symbol of the Deity, a visible object in which its presence would be enshrined, wherein it could be met and wherein its power would be felt at all times.

That religious concern found an ally in one of man's finest skills: the skill to design, to fashion, and to paint in material form what mind and imagination conceive. They became wedded to each other. *Art* became the helpmate of *religion*, and rich was the offspring of that intimate union. It is alone through religion and cult that the consciousness of higher laws could mature and be imposed "upon the individual artist, who would otherwise have given free rein to his imagination, *a style.*" There, in the sanctuary, artists took the first steps toward the sublime. "They learned to eliminate the contingent from form. Types came into being; ultimately the first ideals."[1] Religion and cult inspired the artist to bring forth images full of majesty, magnificent temples and awe-inspiring altars which in turn stirred the heart of the worshiper to greater devotion. What would art have been without the religious sense of mystery and sovereignty, and how dreary would have been religion without the heroic venture of the artist to embody the mysterious in visible forms, to bring his vision out of the darkness of the heart, and to fill the immense absence of the Deity with the light of human genius. The right hand of the artist withers when he forgets the sovereignty of God, and the heart of the religious man has often become dreary without the daring skill of the artist. Art seemed to be the only revelation in the face of the Deity's vast silence.

One is overwhelmed by the sight of the great works of art. They represent in a deep sense man's attempt to celebrate the work of God. God created heaven and earth, and man creates symbols of heaven and symbols of earth. Yet man is not satisfied with the attempt to praise the work of God; he even dares to express the essence of God. God created man, and man creates images of God.

A distinction ought to be made here between *real* and *conventional* symbols. *A real symbol* is a visible object that represents something invisible; something present representing something absent. A real symbol represents, *e.g.,* the Divine because it is assumed that the Divine resides in it or that the symbol partakes to some degree of the reality of the Divine. *A conventional symbol* represents to the mind an entity which is not shown, not because its substance is endowed with something of that entity but because it suggests that entity, by reason of relationship, association or convention, *e.g.,* a flag.

An image is a real symbol. The god and his image are almost identified. They are cherished as the representatives of the gods;

[1] Jacob Burckhardt, *Force and Freedom,* New York, 1943, pp. 191, 318.

118

he who has the image, has the god. It is believed that the god resides in the image or that the image partakes to some degree of the power and reality of the god. A victor nation would carry off the god-image of the conquered nation in order to deprive them of the presence and aid of their god. In the fifteenth century before the common era, a statue of the goddess Ishtar of Nineveh was carried with great pomp and ceremony from Mesopotamia to Egypt, obviously for the purpose of letting Egypt enjoy the blessings which the goddess by her presence would bestow upon the land.[2] As Durkheim remarked, the images of a totem-creature are more sacred than the totem-creature itself. The image may replace the Deity.

The Rejection of the Image

What was the attitude of the prophets toward that grand alliance of religion and art? What is the attitude of the Bible toward the happy union of priest and artist? Did Israel contribute toward cementing that matrimony? Did it use its talents to create worthy symbols of the One God it proclaimed by inspiring its artists to embody in stone the Creator of heaven and earth? Indeed, if a religion is to be judged by the degree to which it contributes to the human need for symbolism, the Decalogue should have contained a commandment, saying: Thou *shalt make* unto thee a symbol, a graven image or some manner of likeness. . . . Instead, the making and worshiping of images was considered an abomination, vehemently condemned in the Bible.[3] If symbolism is the standard, then Moses will have to be accused of having had a retarding influence on the development of man. It is not with a sense of pride that we recall the making of the Golden Calf, nor do we condemn as an act of vandalism the role of Moses in beating it into pieces and grinding it very small, "until

[2]Hugo Winckler, *The Tell-El-Amarna-Letters,* Berlin, 1896, pp. 48 f. J. A. Knudtzon, *Die El-Amarna-Tafeln,* Leipzig, 1915, pp. 178 f. (No. 23), 1050 f.
[3]Cf., for example, Deuteronomy 27:15; Leviticus 4:15.

119

it was as fine as dust" and casting "the dust thereof into the brook that descended out of the mount."

It is perhaps significant that the Hebrew word that came to denote symbol, *semel*, occurs in the Bible five times, but always in a derogatory sense, denoting an idolatrous object.[4]

Nothing is more alien to the spirit of Judaism than the veneration of images. According to an ancient belief, the prophet Elijah, "the angel of the covenant," is present whenever the act of circumcision is performed. To concretize that belief, a vacant chair, called "Elijah's chair," is placed near the seat of the *sandek* (godfather).[5] This is the limit of representation: a vacant chair. To place a picture or statue of the prophet on it, would have been considered absurd as well as blasphemous. To Jewish faith there are no physical embodiments of supreme mysteries. All we have are signs, reminders.

The World Is Not a Symbol

The Second Commandment implies more than the prohibition of images; it implies the rejection of all visible symbols for God; not only of images fashioned by man but also of "any manner of likeness, of any thing that is in heaven above, or that is in the earth beneath, or that is in the water under the earth." The significance of that attitude will become apparent when contrasted with its opposite view.

It would be alien to the spirit of the Bible to assert that the world is a symbol of God. In contrast, the symbolists exhort us: "Neither say that thou hast now no symbol of the Godlike. Is not God's universe a symbol of the Godlike; is not Immensity a Temple?"[6]

4Deuteronomy 4:16; Ezekiel 8:3.5; 2 Chronicles 33:7.15. However, by means of a metathesis, Ibn Ezra finds the word *semel* in *sulam* (ladder); compare his interpretation of Jacob's ladder in his *Commentary* on Genesis 28:11.

5See A. T. Glassberg, *Zikron Berith la-Rishonim*, Berlin, 1892, pp. 176 ff., 231 ff.

6Thomas Carlyle, *Sartor Resartus*, Book III, Chapter 7.

What is the reason for that sharp divergence? To the symbolists, "all visible things are emblems. . . . Matter exists only
spiritually and to represent some idea and body it forth."[7] The
universe is "a mechanism of self-expression for the infinite." The
symbol is but the bodying forth of the infinite, and it is the very
life of the infinite to be bodied forth.[8]

Now, the Bible does not regard the universe as a mechanism
of the self-expression of God. For the world did not come into
being in an act of self-expression but in an act of creation. The
world is not of the essence of God, and its expression is not His.
The world speaks to God, but that speech is not God speaking
to Himself. It would be alien to the spirit of the Bible to say that
it is the very life of God to be bodied forth. The world is neither
His continuation nor His emanation but rather His creation and
possession.

God and Space

The fundamental insight that God is not and cannot be localized in a thing[9] was emphatically expressed at a moment in which
it could have been easily forgotten: at the inauguration of the
Temple in Jerusalem. At that moment Solomon exclaims: "But
will God in very truth dwell on earth? Behold, heaven and the
heaven of heavens cannot contain Thee; how much less this
house that I have built!" (I Kings 8:27). God manifested himself in *events* rather than in *things,* and those events were never
captured or localized in things.

How significant is the fact that Mount Sinai, the place on
which the supreme revelation occurred, did not retain any degree
of holiness! It did not become a shrine, a place of pilgrimage.

The realization that the world and God are not of the same

[7]*Ibidem,* Book I, Chapter 11.

[8]H. F. Dunbar, *Symbolism in Medieval Thought and Its Consummation in
the Divine Comedy,* New Haven, 1929, pp. 15 f.

[9]See A. J. Heschel, *The Sabbath, Its Meaning to Modern Man,* pp. 4 ff.;
"Space, Time, and Reality," *Judaism,* Vol. I, 3, pp. 268 f.

essence is responsible for one of the great revolutions in the spiritual history of man. Things may be *instruments,* never *objects of worship. Matza* (unleavened bread, eaten on Passover), the *shofar* (horn or trumpet for New Year's Day), the *lulav* (the branch of the palm tree used for the festive wreath on the Feast of Booths), are not things to be looked at, to be saluted, to be paid homage to, but things to be used. Being instruments they have symbolic meaning, but they are not primarily regarded as symbols in themselves. A symbol—because of its inherent symbolic quality—is an object of contemplation and adoration.

To a reverent Catholic the cross is a sacred symbol. Gazing at its shape, his mind is drawn into contemplation of the very essence of the Christian faith.

Thomas Aquinas taught that the cross was to be adored with *latria,* i.e., supreme worship, and argued that one might regard a cross or an image in two ways: (1) in itself, as a piece of wood or the like, and so no reverence should be given to a cross or to an image of Jesus; (2) as representing something else, and in this way one may give to the cross *relatively,* i.e., to the cross as carrying the mind to Jesus—the same honor one gives to Jesus *absolutely,* i.e., in Himself. Adoration is also given to the Sacred Heart, as well as to images and relics of the Saints.[10] In contrast, the *image* and *shape* of the scrolls, of a *shofar* or *lulav,* do not convey to us any inspiration beyond reminding us of its function and our obligation.

The spirit of Christian symbolism has shaped the character of church architecture; "a noble church structure may be 'a sermon in stone.'" According to Germanos, the Patriarch of Constantinople (715–730), the church is heaven on earth, the symbol of the Crucifixion, the Entombment, and Resurrection. From the fifth century, symbolism permeated the architecture of the Byzantine church building in all its details. "The sanctuary, the nave and aisles were the sensible world, the upper parts of the church the intelligible cosmos, the vaults the mystical heaven."[11] A

[10]William Edward Addis and T. Arnold, "Latria," *Catholic Dictionary,* 1884, p. 505.

[11]Charles R. Morey, *Medieval Art,* New York, 1942, pp. 104 f.

122

similar spirit is to be found in Western Christianity, where, for example, the shape of church buildings is that of a cross, embodying the basic symbol of Christianity. The altar is often raised three or seven steps, signifying the Trinity or the seven gifts of the Holy Spirit.

In Jewish law which prescribes countless rules for daily living, no directions are given for the shape of a synagogue building.[12] The synagogue is not an abode of the deity but a house of prayer, a gathering place for the people. Entering a synagogue, we encounter no objects designed to impart any particular idea to us. Judaism has rejected the picture as a means of representing ideas; it is opposed to pictographic symbols. The only indispensable object is a Scroll to be read, not to be gazed at.

There is no *inherent* sanctity in Jewish ritual objects. The candelabrum in the synagogue does not represent another candelabrum either in Jerusalem or in heaven. It is not more than you see. It has no symbolic content. According to Jewish law, it is prohibited to imitate the seven-branched candelabrum as well as other features of the Temple in Jerusalem for ritual purposes. "A man may not make a house in the form of the Temple, or an exedra in the form of the Temple hall, or a court corresponding to the Temple court, or a table corresponding to the table [in the Temple] or a candlestick corresponding to the candlestick [in the Temple], but he may make one with five or six or eight lamps, but with seven he should not make, even of other metals [than gold] . . . or even of wood."[13] The anointing oil must not be produced in the same composition to be used outside the Sanctuary. "It is holy and shall be holy unto you" (Exodus 30:32).

The purpose of ritual art objects in Judaism is not to inspire love of God but to enhance our love of doing a *mitzvah* (religious act); to add pleasure to obedience, delight to fulfillment. Thus, the purpose is achieved not in direct contemplation but in combining it with a ritual act; the art objects have a religious function but no religious substance.

[12]Rabbi Yeheskel Landau, *Noda be-Yehudah,* Second Series, Orah Hayim, responsum 19.

[13]*Rosh Hashanah* 24a; *Avodah Zarah* 43a.

Jewish artists often embellished manuscripts and title pages with pictures of Moses and Aaron. Yet such decorations were regarded as ornaments rather than symbols.

Man the Symbol of God

And yet there is something in the world that the Bible does regard as a symbol of God. It is not a temple nor a tree, it is not a statue nor a star. The symbol of God is *man, every man*. God created man in His image (*Tselem*), in His likeness (*demuth*). How significant is the fact that the term *tselem* which is frequently used in a damnatory sense for a man-made image of God, as well as the term *demuth*, of which Isaiah claims (40:18), no *demuth* or likeness can be applied to God—are employed in denoting man as an image and likeness of God.

Human life is holy, holier even than the Scrolls of the Torah. Its holiness is not man's achievement; it is a gift of God rather than attained through merit. Man must, therefore, be treated with the honor due to a likeness representing the King of kings.

Not that the Bible was unaware of man's frailty and wickedness. The Divine in man is not by virtue of what he does but by virtue of what he is. With supreme frankness the failures and shortcomings of kings and prophets, of men such as Moses or David, are recorded. And yet, Biblical tradition insists that not only man's soul but also his body is symbolic of God. This is why even the body of a criminal condemned to death must be treated with reverence, according to the book of Deuteronomy (21:23). He who sheds the blood of a human being, "it is accounted to him as though he diminished or destroyed the Divine image."[14] And in this sense, Hillel characterized the body as an "icon" of God,[15] as it were, and considered keeping clean one's own body an act of reverence for its Creator.[16]

Since not one man or one particular nation but all men of all

[14] *Mekilta* to Exodus 20:16.

[15] *Tselem elohim* in Genesis 1:27 is translated in the Septuagint κατ' εικονα Θεου.

[16] *Leviticus Rabba* 34, 3; see also *Midrash Tehillim*, 103. Significant are the statements in Jer. *Berachoth* III, 8a and *Moed Katan* III, 83a.

124

nations are endowed with the likeness of God, there is no danger of ever worshiping man, because only that which is extraordinary and different may become an object of worship. But the Divine likeness is something all men share.

This is a conception of far-reaching importance to Biblical piety. What it implies can hardly be summarized. Reverence for God is shown in our reverence for man. The fear you must feel of offending or hurting a human being must be as ultimate as your fear of God. An act of violence is an act of desecration. To be arrogant toward man is to be blasphemous toward God.

> He who oppresses the poor blasphemes
> his Maker,
> He who is gracious to the needy
> honors Him.

Proverbs 14:31

"You must not say, since I have been put to shame, let my neighbor be put to shame. . . . If you do so, know whom you put to shame, for in the likeness of God made He him."[17]

Rabbi Joshua ben Levi said: "A procession of angels pass before man when he is travelling, and the heralds proclaim before him, saying: *Make room for the image (eikonion) of God.*"[18]

[17]*Genesis Rabba* 24, 8.

[18]*Deuteronomy Rabba* 4, 4; see *Midrash Tehillim*, Ch. 17. That one lives in the company of angels, "ministers of the Supreme," was something one is expected by *Jewish law* to be always conscious of. This is evidenced by the prayer *hithhabdu, Berachoth* 60b and *Mishne Torah, Tefillah* 7, 4. The general belief, based on Psalms 91:11, is clearly stated in *Taanith* 11a. According to *Exodus Rabba* 32, 6, and *Tanhuma, Mishpatim,* end, angels are assigned to a person according to the good deeds he performs; *Seder Eliahu Rabba,* Ch. XVIII, edition Friedmann, p. 100. Compare also the statement of the two "ministering angels" that accompany a person on Sabbath eve on his way from the synagogue to his home, *Shabbath* 119b. "Rabbi Simeon said: When a man rises at midnight and gets up and studies the Torah till daylight, and when the daylight comes he puts the phylacteries with the holy impress on his head and his arm, and covers himself with his fringed robe, and as he issues from the door of his house he passes the *mezuzah* containing the imprint of the Holy Name on the post of his door, then four holy angels join him and issue with him from the door of his house and accompany him to the synagogue and proclaim before him: Give honor to the image of the Holy King, give honor to the son of the King, to the precious countenance of the King."—*Zohar,* III, p. 265a.

And what is more, Biblical piety may be expressed in the form of a supreme imperative: *Treat yourself as a symbol of God.* In the light of this imperative we can understand the meaning of that astounding commandment: "You shall be holy, for I the Lord your God am holy" (Leviticus 19:2).

It is often claimed that "Hebrew monotheism has ended by raising the deity too far above the earth and placing him too far above man."[19] This is a half-truth. God is indeed very much above man, but at the same time man is very much a reflection of God. The craving to keep that reflection pure, to guard God's likeness on earth, is then the motivating force of Jewish piety.

The *Tselem* or God's image is what distinguishes man from the animal, and it is only because of it that he is entitled to exercise power in the world of nature. If he retains his likeness he has dominion over the beast; if he forfeits his likeness he descends, losing his position of eminence in nature.[20]

The idea of man's divine likeness is, according to one opinion in the Talmud, the reason for the prohibition to produce the human figure. The statement in Exodus 20:20, "You shall not make with Me (*itti*) gods of silver, or gods of gold," should be rendered as if it were written, "You shall not make My symbol (*otti; ot* means symbol), namely, man, gods of silver, or gods of gold."[21]

What is necessary is not *to have a symbol* but *to be a symbol*. In this spirit, all objects and all actions are not symbols in themselves but ways and means of enhancing the living symbolism of man.

The divine symbolism of man is not in what he *has*—such as reason or the power of speech—but in what he *is* potentially: he is able to be holy as God is holy. To imitate God, to act as He acts in mercy and love, is the way of enhancing our likeness.

[19]"It was left for the Christian religion to call down its god from the heights of heaven to earth, and to represent this god by means of art" (A. D. Seta, *Religion and Art,* New York, 1914, p. 148). Indeed, this was not the way of Judaism, which insisted upon its worship being independent of art. It is life itself that must represent the God of Israel.

[20]*Genesis Rabba* 8, 12.

[21]*Abodah Zarah,* 43b.

126

Man becomes what he worships. "Says the Holy One, blessed be He: He who acts like Me shall be like Me." Says Rabbi Levi ben Hama: "Idolaters resemble their idols (Psalms 115:8); now how much more must the servants of the Lord resemble Him."[22]

And yet that likeness may be defiled, distorted, and forfeited. It is from the context of this problem that the entire issue of Jewish symbolism must be considered. The goal of man is to recognize and preserve his likeness or at least to prevent its distortion.

But man has failed. And what is the consequence? "I have placed the likeness of My image on them and through their sins I have upset it," is the dictum of God.[23]

The likeness is all but gone. Today, nothing is more remote and less plausible than the idea that man is a symbol of God. Man forgot Whom he represents or *that* he represents.

There is one hope. The Midrash interprets the verse Deuteronomy 1:10, as if it were written: Lo, today you are like the stars in heaven, but in the future you will resemble the Master.[24]

The likeness of God is broken, yet not utterly destroyed.

II. CONCEPTUAL SYMBOLS

Symbolic Knowledge

Let us now turn to the problem of conceptual symbols. In the last several decades the interest in symbolism has become a decisive trend in our thinking. This is no accident. As long as man believes in his ability to comprehend the world directly, as long as he is impressed by that which *is* rather than concerned to express what he *thinks*, symbolism is one of the techniques of

[22]*Deuteronomy Rabba* 1, 10.
[23]*Moed Katan* 15b.
[24]*Deuteronomy Rabba* 1, 10.

human understanding. When man becomes the measure of good and evil, when truth is regarded as that which the mind creates, symbolism becomes the sole technique of human understanding.

Kant has demonstrated that it is utterly impossible to attain knowledge of the world as it is because knowledge is always in the form of categories and these, in the last analysis, are only representational constructions for the purpose of apperceiving what is given. Objects possessing attributes, causes that work, are all mythical. We can only say that objective phenomena are regarded *as if* they behaved in such and such a way, and there is absolutely no justification for assuming any dogmatic attitude and changing the 'as if' into a 'that.' *Salomon Maimon* was probably the first to sum up Kantian philosophy by saying that only *symbolic knowledge* is possible.[25]

To the contemporary physicist the world of sense-perception is of no relevance whatsoever. The familiar world is abandoned for abstracts, graphs, and equations. His elements are not the familiar phenomena but electrons, quanta, potentials, Hamiltonian functions and the like. Science is purely operational, concerned merely with the manipulation of symbols.

In the light of such a theory, what is the status of religious knowledge? We must, of course, give up the hope ever to attain a valid concept of the supernatural in an objective sense, yet since for practical reasons it is useful to cherish the idea of God, let us retain that idea and claim that while our knowledge of God is not objectively true, it is still *symbolically* true.

Thus, symbolism became the supreme category in understanding religious truth. It has become a truism that religion is largely an affair of symbols. Translated into simpler terms this view regards religion as *a fiction*, useful to society or to man's personal well-being. Religion is, then, no longer a relationship of man to God but a relationship of man to the symbol of his highest ideals: there is no God, but we must go on worshiping His symbol.

[25]See Salomon Maimon, *Versuch ueber die Transcendentalphilosophie,* Berlin, 1790, pp. 29 f.; H. Vaihinger, *The Philosophy of 'As if,'* London, 1935, pp. 29 f.; Friedrich Kuntze, *Die Philosophie Salomon Maimons,* Heidelberg, 1912, pp. 331 f.

The idea of symbolism is, of course, not a modern invention. New only is the role it has now assumed. In earlier times, symbolism was regarded as a form of *religious thinking;* in modern times religion is regarded as *a form of symbolic thinking.*[26]

Symbolism and Solipsism

Is religion the sum of mind plus symbol? Is the mind-symbol relationship the only ultimate form of relationship in which man stands to God? Is symbolic understanding of God all that religion has to offer? If God is a symbol, then religion is a child's play. What is the value of searching for a goal that will for ever remain unknown? Moreover, if God has no mercy and offers no light to those who grope for Him, does He deserve man's desperate efforts to reach Him?

To religion the immediate certainty of faith is more important than all metaphysical reflection, and the pious man must regard religious symbolism as *a form of solipsism,* and just as he who loves a person does not love a symbol or his own idea of the person but the person himself, so he who loves and fears God is not satisfied with worshiping a symbol or worshiping symbolically.

[26]In Hegel's thinking the Absolute in philosophy is identified with the Absolute in religion. There is only truth; only the forms in which the Absolute is grasped are different. The form in religion is that of feeling, of "sensually symbolic ideas," whereas in philosophy the form is that of notion *qua* notion. The symbolic character of religious thinking is never transcended; it is found in the highest or "absolute religion" as well as in "the religion of nature." Symbolic representation of God is cancelled and superseded in the notion which is the form of philosophical thinking and which alone is adequate to convey absolute truth.

Symbols Are Substitutes

Symbols are substitutes, cherished whenever the object we are interested in is momentarily or permanently beyond our reach. Unable to find a direct approach to its object (or a direct way of expressing itself), the mind accepts a symbol in place of the original object of its interest. The premise of religious symbolism is the assumption that God lies beyond the ken of our minds and will, therefore, never be apprehended or expressed directly but only through the symbol. Now the second part of that premise is not logically necessitated by the first. If the knowledge of God is beyond the reach of man, what gives us certainty to assume that there is a symbol that may serve as His representative?

Symbols can be taken seriously only if we are convinced of man's ability to create legitimate symbols, namely, of his ability to capture the invisible in the visible, the absolute in the relative. Their validity will, furthermore, depend upon our being in possession of criteria by means of which we could decide which symbols represent and which misrepresent the object we are interested in; which to accept and which to reject. Yet in order to prove the validity of symbols in general and in order to judge the adequacy of particular symbols, we must be in possession of a knowledge of the symbolized object that is independent of all symbols. To justify and to judge symbols we are in need of *nonsymbolic* knowledge.

Symbols are means of communication. They communicate or convey to us what they represent. Consequently, in order to understand or to appreciate a symbol, we must be in possession of a knowledge of what the symbol stands for. Does not this prove that symbols are secondary to religious knowledge?

And is it conceivable that a religious person would, once he has realized the fictional nature of symbolism, be willing to accept a substitute for God? He will reject not only substitutes for the religious reality but also substitutes for spontaneous expression. Such substitutes distort our vision, stifle our inner life. Giving to symbolic objects what is due to God and directing the soul to express itself by proxy, symbolism degenerates into *a vicarious religion.*

The Will of God Is No Euphemism

Of a violinist who is moving his bow over the strings of his violin we do not say he is performing a symbolic act. Why? Because the meaning of his act is in what he is doing, regardless of what else the act may represent. In rendering a service to a friend, I am not primarily conscious of carrying out an act which should symbolize my friendship; the act *is* friendship. Symbolism is not something that characterizes all aspects of human life. Why are there *no symbols in morality?* Because a moral deed is endowed with intrinsic meaning; its value is in itself, not in what it stands for.

No one eats figuratively, no one sleeps symbolically; so why should the pious man be content to worship God symbolically?

Those who are in the dark in their lonely search for God; those to whom God is a problem, or a Being that is eternally absent and silent; those who ask, "How does one know Him? Where can one find Him? How does one express Him?" will be forced to accept symbols as an answer.

But the Bible is not a religion of an unknown God. It is built upon a rock of certainty that God has made known His will to His people. To us, the will of *God is neither a metaphor nor a euphemism* but more powerful and more real than our own experience.

The Primacy of Literal Meaning

Is, perhaps, the content of the Bible, the manner in which the will of God was made known to man, symbolic?

Reading carefully the words of the Bible, we realize that the essence of Biblical piety is not to be found in the employment of symbols but in something quite different. When the book of Deuteronomy exclaims, "What does the Lord thy God ask of thee?" the answer given is "to fear the Lord thy God, to walk in all His ways, and to serve the Lord thy God with all thy heart and all thy soul, to keep for thy good the commandments of thy Lord and His statutes, which I command you this day" (10:12 f.).

He who loves with all his heart, with all his soul, with all his might, does not love symbolically. Nor does the term "to serve God" refer to a symbolic attitude. The term "service" may be used in two ways: symbolically and literally. When a person is appointed honorary president or honorary secretary of an organization, he is serving symbolically and is not required to carry out any functions. Yet there are others who actually serve an organization or a cause.

What was it that the prophets sought to achieve? To purge the minds of the notion that God desired symbols. The service of God is an extremely concrete, an extremely real, literal, and factual affair. We do not have to employ symbols to make Him understand what we mean. We worship Him not by employing figures of speech but by shaping our actual lives according to His pattern.

The symbolists claim that not the literal meaning of Scripture

132

is the important matter but the spiritual truths hidden beneath it; while Jewish tradition insists, the Biblical commandment must not be divested of *peshat,* of its naked meaning; without the reality of the naked word the spirit is a ghost. Even the mystics who cherished the allegorical meaning of Scripture and regarded the hidden significance as superior to the plain, naked meaning, always insisted that the secret rests upon the plain.

The power of the Bible is in its not being absolutely dependent upon man's symbolic interpretations. The prophets do not live by the grace of preachers. Their words are significant even when taken literally. They do not speak in oracles but in terms of specific actions. *Love thy neighbor as thyself* has a strictly literal meaning, and so has the commandment to observe the Seventh day. The Bible has tried to teach that holiness is vital, that the things of the spirit are real. The Torah is not in heaven. The voice of God is unambiguous; it is the confusion of man, of the best of us, that creates the ambiguity. It tells us precisely how God wants us to act. Performing a sacred deed we are not aware of symbolizing religion; a sacred act *is* religion.

Religious observance has more than two dimensions; it is more than an act that happens between man and an idea. The unique feature of religious living is in its being *three-dimensional.* In a religious act man stands before God. He feels addressed or commanded to act. "Greater is he who acts because he is commanded by God than he who acts without being commanded by Him."[27] Symbolic meaning of an act expresses only what the act means to man in relation to an idea; it does not convey what the act means in relation to God.

Does man stand in a symbolic relation to God? To the outsider, religion may appear as a symbol, just as to those who see a man weep, weeping is a symbol of grief, pain or fear. Yet, to the afflicted man weeping is not a symbol. God was not a symbol to him who exclaimed, "Though He slay me, yet will I trust in Him."[28] Do we pray symbolically? Do we implore Him for symbolic aid?

[27] *Kiddushin* 31a; *Baba Kamma* 38a, 87a.
[28] Job 13:15.

Symbols have their place in the outer court of religion. What is found in the inner sanctuary is neither speculative nor artistic pageantry but the simplicity and immediacy of insight, faith and dedication. There are many symbols in Judaism, but they have auxiliary importance; their status is that of *minhag*.[29] Jewish observance comprises both *mitzvoth* (commandments) and *minhagim* (customs). The Rabbis were careful to distinguish between law and custom.[30] Customs are symbols born of the mind of man; *mitzvoth* are expressions and interpretations of the will of God.

Mitzvoth and Ceremonies

Moses was not concerned with initiating a new cult, but with creating a new people. In the center of Jewish living is not a cult but observance; the former is a realm of its own, the latter comprises all of life. Since the destruction of the Temple in Jerusalem Judaism has had a minimum of cult and a maximum of observance. The prophetic fight against the mendacity of spurious ceremonies has left its trace in our lives. There is a minimum of show, of ceremonialism in Jewish religion, even in public worship. Ceremonies are for the eye, but Judaism is an appeal to the spirit. The only ceremony still observed in the synagogue is the blessing of the priests—but then the congregation is required to close its eyes.

We rarely object to ceremonialism in the observance of state affairs or in courtroom proceedings or to the elaborate ritualism of academic celebrations at American universities. Should we not say that the private and domestic acts must likewise have something that would stamp them as out of the ordinary, and that *mitzvoth* are essentially ceremonies?

Ceremonialism has the pedagogical value of emphasizing the extraordinary character of an occasion. In becoming a daily habit

[29]"Said Abaye: Now that it has been said that symbols are of significance, a man should make a regular habit of eating, at the beginning of the year, pumpkin, fenngreek, leek, beet and dates (these grow in profusion and are symbolic of prosperity)"—*Horayoth* 12a.

[30]*Yebamoth*, 13b; *Niddah* 16a; *Taanith* 26b.

134

it loses its value. A ceremony is an emphasis on a deed. Yet adding an esthetic veneer, decorum, and solemnity, it remains very much on the surface.

A *mitzvah* is performed when a deed is outdone by a sigh, when Divine reference is given to a human fact. In a *mitzvah* we give the source of an act, rather than the underlining of a word. Ceremonies are performed for the sake of onlookers; *mitzvoth* are done for the sake of God. Ceremonies must be visible, spectacular; a *mitzvah* is spurious when turning impressive.

Mitzoth are sanctifications rather than ceremonies. Without faith, the festivities turn dull and artificial. The esthetic satisfaction they offer is meager compared, *e.g.*, with that of listening to a symphony.

The Myth of Self-expression

Symbols are human forms of expression. Yet, is eloquence the essence of piety? Is religion a function of man's power of expression? Is it one of the many dialects of man's language, comparable to art, poetry, and philosophy? The theory that religion is a form of expression is a theory that thinks too much about what man says and ignores the fact that in the face of the ultimate problems he has nothing or very little to say.

The goal of religion is not primarily to help us to express ourselves, but to bring us closer to God. *Empathy* rather than expression is the way of piety. The purpose of *mitzvoth* is not to express ourselves but to expresss the will of God. The most important fact is that God speaks. And he who knows that God speaks cannot regard his own need for speaking and self-expression as being of supreme concern. The supreme concern is how to understand God's speech, God's expression. The *mitzvoth* are words of God which we try to understand, to articulate.

Granted that the need for symbolization is a basic human need, the task of religion would not be to satisfy that need but rather to supply the norms for the right satisfaction of that need. Thus, the essential role of religion would be, if necessary, to prevent certain forms of symbolization. Symbolism may be indigenous to human nature, but religion is more than an aid in the development of the merely human; its goal is to raise the human to the level of the holy.

The primary function of symbols is to express *what we think;* the primary function of the *mitzvoth* is to express *what God wills.* Religious symbolism is *a search for God,* Jewish observance, *a response to God.* In fulfilling the *mitzvoth* our major concern is not to expresss our feelings but to comply, to be in agreeement, with the will of God.

A symbol is a thing, a *mitzvah* is a task. A symbol *is,* a *mitzvah* is an act that *ought to be* done. Symbols have a psychological, not an ontological, status; they do not affect any reality, except the psyche of man. *Mitzvoth* affect God. Symbols evade, *mitzvoth* transcend, reality. Symbols are less, *mitzvoth* are more than real.

Jewish festivals do not contain any attempt to recreate symbolically the events they commemorate. We do not enact the exodus from Egypt nor the crossing of the Red Sea. Decisive as the revelation of Sinai is, there is no ritual to recreate or to dramatize it. We neither repeat nor imitate sacred events. Whatever is done in religious observance is an original act. The Seder ritual, for example, recalls; it does not rehearse the past.

Kavanah and Symbolic Understanding

There was never any doubt that all ritual acts have an ultimate meaning, yet their immediate relevance to us does not lie in their symbolic meaning but in their being commandments of God. Jewish piety demands their fulfillment regardless of whether we comprehend their symbolic meaning. We may not comprehend the wisdom of God, but we are certain of understanding the will of God.

Does the absence of symbolic understanding imply that Jewish observance is nothing but a physical performance? Jewish tradition insists that no performance is complete without the participation of the heart. It asks for the *kavanah,* for inner participation, not only for external action. Yet there is a difference between symbolic understanding and what tradition means by *kavanah.*

Kavanah is awareness of the will of God rather than awareness of the reason of a *mitzvah*. Awareness of symbolic meaning is awareness of a specific idea; *kavanah* is awareness of an ineffable situation. It does not try to appropriate what is part of the divine mystery. It is *kavanah* rather than symbolic understanding that evokes in us ultimate joy at the moment of doing a *mitzvah*.

It is, for example, possible to justify the ritual washing of the hands before a meal as a reminder of a similar priestly ceremony at the Temple in Jerusalem. Yet what is characteristic of Jewish piety is not to be mindful of that reason but to forget all reasons and to make place in the mind for the awareness of God.

Indeed, the certainty of being able to do the will of God lends to the *mitzvoth* a meaning, compared with which all particular explanations seem platitudes. What reason could compete with the claim: This is the will of God?

Moreover, who would be willing to sacrifice his dearest interests observing the Sabbath just because it symbolizes creation or the redemption from Egypt? If the Jews were ever ready for such a sacrifice, it was not because of a symbolic idea but because of God. The ideal of Judaism is to serve for the sake of God, not for the sake of symbols.

The Status of Symbolic Meaning

The validity of a symbol depends upon its intelligibility. An object loses its symbolic character when people forget what it stands for. Yet, in Judaism the knowledge of what the commandments symbolize was not considered essential. *Halacha* has never regarded the understanding of symbolic meaning as a requirement for the proper fulfillment of a *mitzvah*.

The striking fact is that the symbolic meaning of the *mitzvoth* was neither canonized nor recorded. Had such understanding ever been considered essential, how did it happen that the meaning of so many rituals has remained obscure? Had it been known and had its knowledge been regarded as essential, it would not have fallen into oblivion, but would have been transmitted to posterity by a people that so faithfully preserved its heritage.

Let us take an example. On the Feast of Booths we are commanded to carry four kinds of plants. The significance of that ritual is not given in the Bible. So the rabbis offered a symbolic interpretation: The stem of the palm-tree corresponds to the human spine, the leaf of the myrtle to the eye, the willow-leaf to the mouth, and the etrog to the heart.[31] What is the status of that interpretation? It was not claimed to be the authentic original meaning of the ritual. Nor was its awareness considered essential to the fulfillment of the ritual. This particular interpretation is one of several offered. It has devotional meaning.

We must distinguish between that which is *only a symbol* and that which is *also a symbol*. A flag serves only one function, namely, to serve as a symbol; beyond its symbolic function it is a meaningless object. A temple, on the other hand, has a very definite meaning as a building, regardless of its symbolic function. In the same sense, religious observance such as the ritual of the four plants may assume symbolic meaning, it is *also* a symbol, yet its essence is in its being a *mitzvah*.

A system of symbolism implies if not established or canonized meaning, then at least some unanimity of its understanding. The teeming multiplicity of symbolic interpretations of Jewish rituals advanced in the course of the last two thousand years testifies to the fact that symbolic meaning is merely *an afterthought*. No one has succeeded in discovering a system of symbolic meaning by which all *mitzvoth* could be explained with some degree of consistency. The numerous attempts to explore the semantics of the *mitzvoth* have been futile. If Judaism is a system of symbolism, then it must be regarded as a forgotten system.

The essence of Judaism is a demand rather than a creed. It emphasizes the centrality of the act. The act of studying is more important than the possession of knowledge. There is more reflection about the deed than contemplation about the dogma.

Just as an image becomes an idol, a deed may become a habit. Its truthfulness is surrendered when it assumes independence and becomes self-perpetuating and more sacred than God who commanded it.

[31] *Leviticus Rabba*, Ch. 30.

138

The Moment of Meeting

What is the purpose and the justification of symbolism? It is to serve as a *meeting place* of the spiritual and the material, of the invisible and the visible. Judaism, too, had such a meeting place—in a qualified sense—in the Sanctuary. Yet in its history the point of gravity was shifted from space to time, and instead of a place of meeting came *a moment of meeting;* the meeting is not in a thing but in a deed.

Ritual acts are moments which man shares with God, moments in which man identifies himself with the will of God. Symbols are detached from one's being; they are apart from the soul. Yet, God asks for the heart, not for the symbol; he asks for deeds, not for ceremonies.

Symbolism and the Sense of the Ineffable

Essential to human thought is not only the technique of symbolization but also *the awareness of the ineffable.*[32] In every mind there is an enormous store of not-knowing, of being puzzled, of wonder, of *radical amazement.* While the mind manufactures ideas, translating insights into symbols, the deeper knowledge remains: what *is* we cannot say.

Thus, what characterizes man is not only his ability to develop words and symbols, but also his being compelled to draw a distinction between the utterable and the unutterable, to be stunned by that which is and cannot be put into words. It is *the sense of the ineffable* that we have to regard as the root of man's creative activities in art, thought and noble living. The attempt to convey what we see and cannot say is the everlasting theme of mankind's unfinished symphony, a venture in which adequacy is never achieved. There is an eternal disparity between the ultimate and man's power of expression.

Science does not know the world as it is; it knows the world in human terms. Scientific knowledge is symbolic knowledge.

[32] A. J. Heschel, *Man Is Not Alone,* pp. 3 ff.

Trying to hold an interview with reality face to face, without the aid of human terms or symbols, we realize that what is intelligible to our mind is but a thin surface of the profoundly undisclosed.

The awareness of the unknown is earlier than the awareness of the known. Next to our mind are not names, words, symbols, but the nameless, the inexpressible, being. It is otherness, remoteness upon which we come within all our experience.

Just as the simple-minded equates appearance with reality, so does the overwise equate the expressible with the ineffable, the symbolic with the metasymbolic.

Philosophy and Religion

The awareness of the ineffable, of the metasymbolic, is that with which our search must begin. Philosophy, enticed by the promise of the known, has often surrendered the treasures of higher incomprehension to poets and mystics, although without the sense of the ineffable there are no metaphysical problems, no awareness of being as being, of value as value.

A recent publication which undertook to analyze the concept of value concludes with the following statement:

"Our essay has ended with the unsayable. We cannot in a correct language formulate an answer to our question: What is value? . . . Should we not give up the whole undertaking as unnecesssarily self-frustrating? I think not. I need not and I shall not conceal the fact that I have my own moments of despondency when I am tempted to throw aside the whole philosophical endeavour to find an answer to such questions as, What is value? What is fact? What is truth? What is entailment? What is designation? And I suspect that this despondency is not peculiar to me and my individual inadequacies as a philosopher; I suspect that everyone who has seriously wrestled with these issues must have at some time experienced it. . . .

"It is not then to be wondered at that we end with the unsayable: This we should expect. The objective should be to postpone this inevitable result as long as possible, to push the unsayable as far back as we can, to let the object speak for itself only

140

after we have said as much as can be said to bring out what is not obvious.

"If the present essay has been successful in postponing ultimate taciturnity for a few thousand words, this is the only sort of success its author could realistically have aimed at, always providing that this postponement has not destroyed or signally lessened the final vision. . . . Nothing can be done, save to return constantly to the task of pushing the obvious further back. . . .

"This whole appeal to the obvious, to the revelation of what cannot be said, as the ultimate arbiter of philosophic disputes may be disconcerting to some prosaic minds. It smacks too much of mysticism, but it is mysticism in its most plebeian and I hope unobjectionable garb. There is meant no escape to some ecstatic experience, some high, emotional plane achieved only by the few on rare occasions. The vision appealed to is that which is obvious in all experience, and which is revealed in the sense of our everyday language, a sense that is felt by everyone using that language in everyday situations.

"It is hoped that this essay has met this test, that it has not only postponed by some two-hundred-odd pages the appeal to the obvious (in this sense), but, resting finally on this appeal, really has retained the obvious, that it has remained true to our feelings for everyday language in pushing back into the unsayable but seen an answer to the question, What is value?"[33]

This is the difference between religion and philosophy. Religion *begins* with the sense of the ineffable; philosophy *ends* with the sense of the ineffable. Religion begins where philosophy ends.

Symbolism and Immediacy

A symbol is by definition not the ultimate; it is the representative of something else. What is ultimate is not translated into symbols; the ultimate is an antonym of the symbolic.

We must distinguish between *symbolic knowledge* which we obtain through logical operations, such as analysis and syllogism;

[33]Everett W. Hall, *What Is Value? An Essay in Philosophical Analysis*, New York, The Humanities Press; London, Routledge and Kegan Paul, Ltd., 1952, pp. 247–248.

141

and *immediate understanding* which enables us to acquire insights which are not derived from symbols but from an intimate engagement with what is real. Insights such as the meaning of joy or the difference between beauty and ugliness or the awareness of temporality, of the transitoriness of existence, we do not acquire through the mediation of symbols but through direct acquaintance.

The soul of the religious man lives in the depth of certainty: This is what God wants me to do. Where that certainty is dead, the most powerful symbolism will be futile.

The Clamor for Symbols

The whole history of religion is filled with the struggle between the pursuit of idols and the worship of Him whose name is ineffable; *between symbolic knowledge and metasymbolic understanding;* between employing symbols *as means* and accepting them *as ends.* In the past, symbols have often served as substitutes for insight, for immediate perception; as an alibi for faith. The need for symbolism does not always rise when the power to pray increases. When in medieval Christianity symbolism threatened to smother the immediacy of faith, the Reformation raised its voice against it. Today there is a clamor for symbolism perceptible both in Jewish and Christian circles.

Is the present-day cry for symbols a cry for God? Is the craving for ceremonies an expression of a more profound care for the will of God? These are the questions our critical sense must ask.

Symbolism — a Trap

Symbolism is so alluring because it promises to rehabilitate beliefs and rituals that have become meaningless to the mind. Yet, what it accomplishes is to reduce belief to make-believe, observance to ceremony, prophecy to literature, theology to esthetics.

Symbols are esthetic objects: either things to be looked at that please the senses and demand nothing in return, or ideas that offer enjoyment without involving us in ultimate commitments. A symbol is often like a plaything, an imitation of reality, cherished for the emotional satisfaction it affords. Symbolism, indeed, is an esthetic category.

The quest for symbols is a *trap* for those who seek the truth. Symbols may either distort what is literally true or profane what is ineffably real. They may, if employed in the inner chamber of the mind, distort our longing for God into mere esthetics.

When their meaning becomes stale, symbols die. But what is worse, the heart of faith dies of an overdose of symbolism. It is better that symbols die and faith should live.

Symbolism undermines the certainty of history, implying that even God did not succeed in conveying His will to us, and that we did not succeed in understanding His will. Man speaks in symbols; God speaks in events and commands.

Realizing all this, one begins to wonder whether symbolism is an authentic category of prophetic religion. Or whether it is not a device of higher apologetics, a method of rationalization?

The uniqueness of the Bible is not in its symbolism. The religions of Egypt, Rome, India were rich in symbolism; what they lacked was not the symbol but the knowledge of *"the living God."* The uniquenesss of the Bible is in disclosing the will of God in plain words, in telling us of the presence of God in history rather than in symbolic signs or mythic events. The mysterious ladder which Jacob saw was a dream; the redemption of Israel from Egypt was an iron fact. The ladder was in the air, while Jacob's head was on a stone.

A New Heart or New Symbols

"You do not believe, said Coleridge; you only believe that you believe. It is the final scene in all kinds of worship and symbolism."[34]

[34]Carlyle, *Heroes and Hero-worship,* IV (1841), p. 198.

Let us never forget: *If God is a symbol, He is a fiction.* But if *God is real*, then He is able to express His will unambiguously. Symbols are makeshifts, necessary to those who cannot express themselves unambiguously.

There is darkness in the world and horror in the soul. What is it that the world needs most? Will man-made symbols redeem humanity? In the past, wars have been waged over differences in symbols rather than over differences in the love of God. Symbols, ceremonies are by their very nature particularistic. Symbols separate us, insights unite us. They unite us regardless of the different ways in which they are expressed. What we need is honesty, stillness, humility. What we need is a *new insight* rather than new symbols.

Symbols without faith are unnecessary baggage. Our task is to overcome the callousness of soul, to be led to a plane where no one can remain both callous and calm; where His presence may be defied but not denied, and where, at the end, faith in Him is the only way.

What we ought to strive for is to find out whether we have a common concern, whether, *e.g.*, we are interested in atonement at all. Then the question of what symbols express atonement is secondary. What we need is *immediacy*. The ultimate human need is the need for a meaning of existence. This will not be found through introducing a set of symbols.

To repeat: harsh and bitter are the problems which religion comes to solve: ignorance, evil, malice, power, agony and despair. These problems cannot be solved through generalities, through philosophical symbols. Our problem is: Do we believe what we confess? Do we mean what we say?

We do not suffer symbolically; we suffer literally, truly, deeply; symbolic remedies are quackery. The will of God is either real or a delusion.

This is our problem: We have eyes to see but see not; we have ears to hear but hear not (Ezekiel 12:2). There is God, and we do not understand Him; there is His word and we ignore it. This is the problem for us. Any other issue is relevant as far as it helps us solve that challenge.

144

6

The Meaning
of This Hour

The Meaning of This Hour[1]

Emblazoned over the gates of the world in which we live is the escutcheon of the demons. The mark of Cain in the face of man has come to overshadow the likeness of God. There has never been so much guilt and distress, agony, and terror. At no time has the earth been so soaked with blood. Fellowmen turned out to be evil ghosts, monstrous and weird. Ashamed and dismayed, we ask: Who is responsible?

History is a pyramid of efforts and errors; yet at times it is

[1]The essential part of this essay was originally delivered in March 1938 at a conference of Quaker leaders in Frankfurt-am-Main, Germany. It was expanded and published in 1943. It is printed here with a few modifications.

147

the Holy Mountain on which God holds judgment over the nations. Few are privileged to discern God's judgment in history. But all may be guided by the words of the Baal Shem: If a man has beheld evil, he may know that it was shown to him in order that he learn his own guilt and repent; for what is shown to him is also within him.

We have trifled with the name of God. We have taken the ideals in vain. We have called for the Lord. He came. And was ignored. We have preached but eluded Him. We have praised but defied Him. Now we reap the fruits of our failure. Through centuries His voice cried in the wilderness. How skillfully it was trapped and imprisoned in the temples! How often it was drowned or distorted! Now we behold how it gradually withdraws, abandoning one people after another, departing from their souls, despising their wisdom. The taste for the good has all but gone from the earth. Men heap spite upon cruelty, malice upon atrocity.

The horrors of our time fill our souls with reproach and everlasting shame. We have profaned the word of God, and we have given the wealth of our land, the ingenuity of our minds and the dear lives of our youth to tragedy and perdition. There has never been more reason for man to be ashamed than now. Silence hovers mercilessly over many dreadful lands. The day of the Lord is a day without the Lord. Where is God? Why didst Thou not halt the trains loaded with Jews being led to slaughter? It is so hard to rear a child, to nourish and to educate. Why dost Thou make it so easy to kill? Like Moses, we hide our face; for we are afraid to look upon *Elohim*, upon His power of judgment. Indeed, where were we when men learned to hate in the days of starvation? When raving madmen were sowing wrath in the hearts of the unemployed?

Let modern dictatorship not serve as an alibi for our conscience. We have failed to fight *for* right, *for* justice, *for* goodness; as a result we must fight *against* wrong, *against* injustice, *against* evil. We have failed to offer sacrifices on the altar of peace; thus we offered sacrifices on the altar of war. A tale is told of a band of inexperienced mountain climbers. Without guides, they struck

148

recklessly into the wilderness. Suddenly a rocky ledge gave way beneath their feet and they tumbled headlong into a dismal pit. In the darkness of the pit they recovered from their shock only to find themselves set upon by a swarm of angry snakes. Every crevice became alive with fanged, hissing things. For each snake the desperate men slew, ten more seemed to lash out in its place. Strangely enough, one man seemed to stand aside from the fight. When indignant voices of his struggling companions reproached him for not fighting, he called back: If we remain here, we shall be dead before the snakes. I am searching for a way of escape from the pit for all of us.

Our world seems not unlike a pit of snakes. We did not sink into the pit in 1939, or even in 1933. We had descended into it generations ago, and the snakes have sent their venom into the bloodstream of humanity, gradually paralyzing us, numbing nerve after nerve, dulling our minds, darkening our vision. Good and evil, that were once as real as day and night, have become a blurred mist. In our every-day life we worshiped force, despised compassion, and obeyed no law but our unappeasable appetite. The vision of the sacred has all but died in the soul of man. And when greed, envy and the reckless will to power came to maturity, the serpents cherished in the bosom of our civilization broke out of their dens to fall upon the helpless nations.

The outbreak of war was no surprise. It came as a long expected sequel to a spiritual disaster. Instilled with the gospel that truth is mere advantage and reverence weakness, people succumbed to the bigger advantage of a lie—"the Jew is our misfortune"—and to the power of arrogance—"tomorrow the whole world shall be ours," "the peoples' democracies must depend upon force." The roar of bombers over Rotterdam, Warsaw, London, was but the echo of thoughts bred for years by individual brains, and later applauded by entire nations. It was through our failure that people started to suspect that science is a device for exploitation; parliaments pulpits for hypocrisy, and religion a pretext for a bad conscience. In the tantalized souls of those who had faith in ideals, suspicion became a dogma and contempt the only solace. Mistaking the abortions of their conscience for intellectual heroism, many thinkers employ clever pens to scold and to scorn the reverence for life, the awe for truth, the loyalty to justice. Man, about to hang himself, discovers it is easier to hang others.

The conscience of the world was destroyed by those who were wont to blame others rather than themselves. Let us remember. We revered the instincts but distrusted the prophets. We labored to perfect engines and let our inner life go to wreck. We ridiculed superstition until we lost our ability to believe. We have helped to extinguish the light our fathers had kindled. We have bartered holiness for convenience, loyalty for success, love for power, wisdom for information, tradition for fashion.

We cannot dwell at ease under the sun of our civilization as our ancestors thought we could. What was in the minds of our martyred brothers in their last hours? They died with disdain and scorn for a civilization in which the killing of civilians could become a carnival of fun, for a civilization which gave us mastery over the forces of nature but lost control over the forces of our self.

Tanks and planes cannot redeem humanity, nor the discovery of guilt by association nor suspicion. A man with a gun is like a beast without a gun. The killing of snakes will save us for the moment but not forever. The war has outlasted the victory of arms as we failed to conquer the infamy of the soul: the indifference to crime, when committed against others. For evil is indivisible. It is the same in thought and in speech, in private and in social life. The greatest task of our time is to take the souls of men out of the pit. The world has experienced that God is involved. Let us forever remember that the sense for the sacred is as vital to us as the light of the sun. There can be no nature without spirit, no world without the Torah, no brotherhood without a father, no humanity without attachment to God.

God will return to us when we shall be willing to let Him in— into our banks and factories, into our Congress and clubs, into our courts and investigating committees, into our homes and theaters. For God is everywhere or nowhere, the Father of all men or no man, concerned about everything or nothing. Only in His presence shall we learn that the glory of man is not in his will to power, but in his power of compassion. Man reflects either the image of His presence or that of a beast.

Soldiers in the horror of battle offer solemn testimony that life is not a hunt for pleasure, but an engagement for service; that there are things more valuable than life; that the world is not a vacuum. Either we make it an altar for God or it is invaded by demons. There can be no neutrality. Either we are ministers of the sacred or slaves of evil. Let the blasphemy of our time not become an eternal scandal. Let future generations not loathe us for having failed to preserve what prophets and saints, martyrs and scholars have created in thousands of years. The apostles of force have shown that they are great in evil. Let us reveal that we can be as great in goodness. We will survive if we shall be as fine and sacrificial in our homes and offices, in our Congress and clubs as our soldiers are on the fields of battle.

There is a divine dream which the prophets and rabbis have cherished and which fills our prayers, and permeates the acts of true piety. It is the dream of a world, rid of evil by the grace of God as well as by the efforts of man, by his dedication to the task of establishing the kingship of God in the world. God is waiting for us to redeem the world. We should not spend our life hunting for trivial satisfactions while God is waiting constantly and keenly for our effort and devotion.

The Almighty has not created the universe that we may have opportunities to satisfy our greed, envy and ambition. We have not survived that we may waste our years in vulgar vanities. The martyrdom of millions demands that we consecrate ourselves to the fulfillment of God's dream of salvation. Israel did not accept the Torah of their own free will. When Israel approached Sinai, God lifted up the mountain and held it over their heads, saying: "Either you accept the Torah or be crushed beneath the mountain."

The mountain of history is over our heads again. Shall we renew the covenant with God?